The Oxford
of
Inspector Morse

Antony Richards
Philip Attwell

All correspondence for
The Oxford of Inspector Morse
should be addressed to:

Irregular Special Press
Endeavour House
170 Woodland Road
Sawston
Cambridgeshire
CB22 3DX

❀❀❀❀ ⭕ ❀❀❀❀

❀❀❀❀❀ ⭕ ❀❀❀❀❀

Cover Illustration: Morse and Lewis pose beside the famous Jaguar at Merton Field with Merton College and the appropriately named path, Dead Man's Walk, in the background. (© Rex Features)

❀❀❀❀❀ ⭕ ❀❀❀❀❀

❀❀❀❀❀ ⭕ ❀❀❀❀❀

Proof reading by Roger Johnson

CONTENTS

Contents

4

FOREWORD

Suppose you are a psychologist in 1974 and try a word association exercise with a group of people. The word *Oxford* is mentioned and you wait for a response. The association you obtain in reply might be some aspect of the University of Oxford, the annual Oxford & Cambridge boat race, the Oxford English Dictionary, Oxford dark blue, Oxford shoes, Oxford marmalade or even the Oxford Movement – to give just a few examples of the great variety of things linked with this fine city. Ask the same question a year later, after the publication of *Last Bus to Woodstock*, the first Inspector Morse novel, or in 1987, after the first television adaptation had been screened, and almost certainly a large number of people would instantly associate Oxford with Chief Inspector Morse of the Thames Valley Police.

A similar word association exercise may be played with the word *Morse* itself. Here, one might expect people to think of Morse code, with far fewer knowing that it was named after Samuel Finlay Breeze Morse, the American inventor of the recording telegraph, and also an artist of some acclaim. A very small number of people may name Jeremy Morse, the ex-chairman of Lloyds Bank (after whom Chief Inspector Morse was named), but today almost everyone would know of the aforementioned Chief Inspector Morse created by Colin Dexter. Such is the power of television and the written word that the many centuries of colourful history that Oxford has enjoyed amount to practically nothing compared with a fictional creation from the 1970s.

The reason for this sensation is several fold. First the medium of television is a powerful one, especially if the programme produced is perceived to be of good quality, and the Inspector Morse adaptations certainly fall into this category, as do the more recent *Lewis* and *Endeavour* episodes. Another reason lies in the writing of the books, which are characterised by being well researched, with complex yet intelligent plots, while still being highly readable to people the world over whether in bed, on a long journey, or just relaxing in the sun on holiday. The character of Morse himself is one that strikes an immediate empathy in many and sympathy in others. There is a little piece of Morse in us all, or at least in somebody we all know, and this is the great attraction of the man brought to life on the small screen in the excellent portrayal by the late John Thaw.

However, Morse is nothing without Lewis, just as Holmes is nothing without Watson, and so much credit must also go to Kevin Whately for his splendid characterisation of Sergeant (and now Inspector) Lewis.

Then there are the cameo parts, each of which contributes to the whole and would be sadly missed by the expectant viewers. An *Inspector Morse* episode just wouldn't be right without Superintendent Strange, or a pathologist (whether it be the reticent Max, or the rather attractive Grayling Russell and Laura Hobson) or of course watching for that fleeting Hitchcock-like appearance from Colin Dexter himself.

Two other aspects whose role in the success of the *Inspector Morse* series should not be undervalued are his Jaguar Mk. II car and the backdrop provided by Oxford itself, although much of the filming was done elsewhere. For example it is no good trying to search out the film location of Morse's flat in Oxford for it is actually located in Ealing, London which substitutes admirably for the fine residences in North Oxford, as do parts of Uxbridge in the more recent *Lewis* series.

This booklet surveys some of the best known and interesting Oxford locations used in the novels and television adaptations from a historical perspective. It is by no means an 'A-Z of Morse' or a history of Oxford but very much intended for the general reader. Indeed, it was originally published to accompany the very first Inspector Morse Society weekend held in Oxford during October 1997. It is pleasing to see that this booklet has been revised and reprinted a number of times and has even appeared in the Blackwell books bestsellers list (at number six). We hope that you have as much fun reading this publication as we did compiling it for our members.

Antony Richards
Philip Attwell

INTRODUCTION

The 6th January has several notable events associated with it. It was on this date that Harold was crowned King of England in succession to Edward the Confessor (1066), the day that King Alfred defeated the Danes at the Battle of Ashdown (871), the alleged birthday of Sherlock Holmes and the day on which Samuel Finlay Breeze Morse gave the first public demonstration of the electric telegraph (1838).

In view of the latter two anniversaries it was entirely appropriate that on Tuesday 6th January 1987 television viewers in Great Britain were introduced to the first adaptation of an Inspector Morse novel, *The Dead of Jericho*. In fact the first novel, *Last Bus to Woodstock*, was published twelve years earlier by Colin Dexter and was the result of a rainy holiday in Wales during 1972. Colin is a teacher by profession, having graduated from Cambridge in 1953 where he was a Latin and Greek scholar. While a school teacher he wrote several books on general studies and politics. In 1966 he moved to Oxford and worked for the University Examination Board. Although retired since 1988, he still worked part-time for the Board during the summer months for some years.

The idea of a crime novel was something of a departure. It was started originally to relieve the boredom of the holiday in Wales, and was finished one page at a time, after listening to *The Archers*, each evening at home, during the following months. The story was first offered for publication to Collins, who must now be sorry that they rejected it. Macmillan had more faith and printed it, but even so it wasn't an instant hit until the character was introduced to the public on the television screen. Incidentally, the name for the now famous detective came from Sir Jeremy Morse, the ex-chairman of Lloyds Bank. In fact it is entirely in keeping with the character, for Morse is an old Oxford name and Sir Jeremy Morse, like his fictional counterpart, is also an inveterate crossword solver. The character is also semi-autobiographical in nature, for Colin Dexter also has a passion for Wagner, crosswords, beer and women.

An area the books score well in is the topographical detail of Oxford, while, if there is a weakness, it is in how strict police procedure is often ignored for the sake of flow in the writing. The television series did impose some changes as well. For instance Morse now drives a Jaguar, whereas in the books he originally drove a Lancia.

The first two series were based on Colin Dexter books, but from series three onwards he took a more background role by writing the plots and adjusting scripts so as not to destroy the original characterisation. This continues right up to the present day for Colin was very much involved with the script editing of the new *Lewis* and *Endeavour* episodes.

His twelve Inspector Morse novels (and one set of short stories) are highly acclaimed, with *The Way Through the Woods* and *The Wench is Dead* awarded Gold Daggers by the Crime Writers Association for best crime novel of the year. He has also been awarded Silver Daggers for *Service of All the Dead* and *The Dead of Jericho*. The accolades keep coming and on 6th October 2008 Colin won the Classic Television Drama writer's award at the ITV3 Crime Thriller Awards, an especially important award since it was voted upon by a public telephone poll.

THE OXFORD OF INSPECTOR MORSE

During twenty-five years of filming thirty-three episodes of *Inspector Morse*, six series of *Lewis* and most recently *Endeavour*, well over a hundred different Oxford city centre locations have been used. However, many of these were as backdrops or fill-ins to the series and only seen fleetingly in passing. Those places outlined here have been chosen because they either played a pivotal role in an episode or book, or because the location presents a point of interest in itself which should also appeal to interest to the general reader. For example only a dozen or so of the many colleges used in filming are mentioned here, and although it is tempting to review all the Morse-related public houses the list has been restricted to just the most well known. There are other books in the **References** section that go into the minutiae of *Inspector Morse* filming that are recommended for the ardent enthusiast. The following are all within walking distance of the Oxford Tourist Information Centre in Broad Street and are listed alphabetically for convenience, but by far the best way of exploring the Oxford of Inspector Morse is to take the circular walking tour as outlined in this guide.

ASHMOLEAN MUSEUM

[The Ashmolean Museum, formally the Taylor Institute]

The Museum is named after Elias Ashmole, a friend of the Tradescant family whose collection of rarities, known as Tradescant's Ark, was in the 17th century considered one of the best of its type in the world. The collection was opened to the public in Lambeth and included beasts, fowls, fishes, serpents, coins, shells, feathers, carvings, paintings, flora, weapons, shoes, Chinese lanterns and Red Indian hunting shirts, to name but a few of the subjects covered. In 1659, three years before his death, John Tradescant made over the collection to Ashmole by a deed of gift, but must have regretted this for in his will he stated that the collection should go to the university of either Cambridge or Oxford. Further the collection was to remain the possession of Mrs. Tradescant while she lived, and it was left up to her to decide which of the universities should receive the gift.

Ashmole disputed the will for over ten years and even took a lease on the house next door to Mrs. Tradescant. The deciding factor was when it transpired that Mrs. Tradescant had been selling off pieces from the collection against her husband's wishes. Ashmole's claim was upheld and following an attempted burglary the collection was moved to Ashmole's house. Shortly afterwards Mrs. Tradescant was found drowned in her garden pond. Maybe this is another case such as *The Wench is Dead* that Inspector Morse should have investigated retrospectively?

Ashmole gave the collection, including various items of his own, to the University of Oxford on condition that a suitable building be found in which to display the items. The first Ashmolean Museum was in Broad Street where much of the collection was neglected for most of the 18th century. However, by the 19th century the University also had other collections of a similar nature which it did not know how to display. This included items from the Bodleian Library, a bequest of prints and drawings from Francis Douce, ancient marbles bequeathed by John Selden and further marbles from the Arundel Collection.

A new neo-classical building in Beaumont Street, designed by Charles Robert Cockerell, was opened in 1845 and became the new Ashmolean Museum (with the east wing housing the Taylor Institution named after Sir Robert Taylor who left the residue of his estate to enable the creation of a foundation for the teaching of modern European languages). The picture gallery on the first floor was named after one of the principal benefactors of the building, the Reverend Dr. Francis Randolph, who also gave his name to the famous hotel opposite. Other bequests followed which brought drawings by Raphael and Michelangelo, watercolours by Turner and the painting of *The Hunt* by Uccello. In 1894 a large extension was added which was funded by a large donation made by C. D. E. Fortnum. Meanwhile what survived of Tradescant's collection was moved to the University Museum, while other items of ethnographical significance were relocated to the Pitt Rivers Museum.

In 1899 the name Ashmolean Museum was applied to the new extension, while the old Ashmolean Museum became the Museum of the History of Science. The Heberden Coin Room was opened in 1922 and a gallery for the Cast Collection in 1960. Two years later the Oriental Collections from the Indian Institute were also added to the Ashmolean Museum.

Between 2006 and 2009 the museum was expanded to cover five floors, virtually doubling the public viewing areas, and includes a new education centre and roof-top restaurant (which features in *Lewis: Fearful Symmetry*). The museum contains many noteworthy exhibits including the Alfred Jewel, Guy Fawkes's lantern, the Stradivari violin *Le Messie* and pictures by Holbein, Bellini, Titian, Van Dyke, Rubens, Rembrandt, Poussin, Gainsborough, Blake, Constable, Manet, Pissarro, Degas, van Gogh, Picasso and several Pre-Raphaelites.

[The Alfred Jewel]

The Wolvercote Tongue (which later became the novel *The Jewel that was Ours*) was based on the Alfred Jewel, an Anglo-Saxon gem consisting of a cloisonné enamel plaque set under a large rock salt crystal with a gold mount. It has an inscription (*Aelfred mec heht gewyrcan*) reading (in translation) 'Alfred ordered me to be made'. No other artefact surviving from that era embodies so many rich resonances as this unique piece of goldsmith's work. It was found in 1693 in a field in North Petherton, Somerset close to Athelney Abbey from where King Alfred launched a counter-attack on the Danes, which ultimately led to their defeat at Edington in 878. It was given to the museum in 1718.

The purpose of the jewel is not known, there being speculation as to whether is was part of the then crown jewels (being part of the royal headdress), or maybe a pendant, or most probably (according to modern thought) an *aestel* (a pointer used to follow the gospel texts). Whatever its use the jewel is incomplete, which fits in well with the story line of *The Jewel that was Ours*.

The Wolvercote Tongue was to be one of the treasures in the Ashmolean Museum, largely due to the efforts of Dr. Theodore Kemp. However, before the handing over of the jewel, its owner Laura Stratton (Poindexter in the television version) dies, the Wolvercote Tongue goes missing and the case begins ...

Lewis and Hathaway visit the museum in *Lewis: Whom the Gods Would Destroy* and examine a four-drachma coin. Hathaway tries to explain the connection between the coin, Nietzsche and Dionysus (the god of wine and celebration) who will later provide a critical clue in this case. The museum again featured, albeit in passing, in both *Lewis: And the Moonbeams Kiss the Sea* and *Lewis: The Great and the Good*, but also rather more prominently in *Lewis: The Point of Vanishing* where a painting provides Lewis with a vital insight into what is a convoluted plot, though one wonders if Inspector Morse would have been as slow in making the same connection. More recently both the interior and exterior were featured in *Lewis: Wild Justice* and *Lewis: Fearful Symmetry* (as this is where the *Marion Hammond: Fallen* exhibition is being held).

BEAR INN

Originally known as Parne Hall, it was burnt down in 1421, rebuilt as Le Tabard which in 1432 became the Bear Inn. The bear and ragged staff were the emblems of Richard Neville, Earl of Warwick. The Inn became one of the largest taverns in Oxford by the middle of the 16th century with royal commissions and circuit judges meeting there regularly. In 1586 Lord Norris and his suite were attacked at the Bear Inn by University scholars as a reprisal against imprisonment of Magdalen men who had stolen deer from Shotover Royal Forest.

[The Bear Inn as it is today]

The Bear Inn became a coaching inn during the 18th century and was the home of the famous 'Oxford Machine' coach. In 1801 it closed. The present Bear Inn was an ostler's house which was attached to the older premises in 1606, and subsequently became the Jolly Trooper in 1774, and the Bear Inn in 1801 after the closure of the original much larger inn, which had thirty rooms and stabling for thirty horses. Today the premise houses a famous collection of ties begun in 1952 by the then landlord, Alan Course.

In the chase scene in *Absolute Conviction* Charlie Bennett, the prisoner, evades Lewis by dodging through the Bear Inn and going up Wheatsheaf Passage to High Street. Morse visits the Bear Inn in *Death is now My Neighbour* for some refreshment and to identify a tie from the pub's massive collection. He fails in this endeavour but is then helped by the landlady who tells him that she has seen the exact same tie on sale at Marks & Spencer.

BLACKWELL'S BOOKSHOP

[Blackwell's bookshop in Broad Street today (left)
and as depicted in a 1926 advertisement (right)]

Benjamin Henry Blackwell was the founder of this world-famous bookshop in 1879. It has always been located in Broad Street and has always been a family business and a private company. In the beginning the shop dealt almost exclusively with second-hand books. In 1883 Blackwell bought the freehold to the shop and moved from Holywell Street to live above the premises. In time the enterprise expanded and the adjacent buildings were also bought.

In 1924 Benjamin Blackwell died and was succeeded by his son, Basil, as company chairman. Later he became Sir Basil but to those in the trade he was always known as 'the Gaffer'. It was he who promoted the publishing side of the business. First there was an annual series of *Oxford Poetry* followed in 1919 by the magazine *Oxford Outlook*. Dorothy L. Sayers was his first editorial assistant.

Basil's son, Richard, joined the firm in 1946 when the annual turnover was one hundred and sixty-five thousand pounds. Today it is closer to one hundred million pounds. The increase in sales meant an increase in space required to house the books. The children's department moved further down Broad Street to No. 22, later to No. 6 and in 1986 to No. 8 where it is today. A paperback shop was opened at Nos. 23-25 Broad Street along with an art and poster shop at No. 27 Broad Street. However, this did not alleviate the problem of space for the core business, so in 1966 the main shop moved underground. An enormous terraced chamber was constructed under the southeast corner of Trinity College. The room has three miles of shelving and at the time found itself in the *Guinness Book of Records* for having the largest display of books for sale in one room anywhere in the world. In 1970 the music shop opened on a site in Holywell Street belonging to Wadham College and shared by the rare books department. Three further specialist shops dealing with medical texts, university textbooks and maps/travel books may be found at the John Radcliffe Hospital, Oxford Brookes University and at No. 53 Broad Street respectively.

In the television adaptation of *Service of all the Dead* Morse is seen looking in the window of Blackwell's in Broad Street, while in *The Daughters of Cain* Morse and Lewis park outside the shop on their return from Leicester and their visit to Mary Rodway to talk about her son's drug-related suicide. Also in *Who Killed Harry Field?* Morse is seen to park his Jaguar in Broad Street prior to entering the bookshop. The inside of Blackwell's Music shop is used for an interview in *Lewis: Music to Die For*, while the exterior of the bookshop is used in *Lewis: Allegory of Love*.

BOATHOUSES

The Oxford University Boat Club was founded on 23rd April 1839 with the prime function of producing crews for the annual Oxford & Cambridge boat race, and for many years, along with Cambridge, was also the foundation of the British Olympic rowing teams. In the five years to 1984 Oxford oarsmen won six Olympic and world-championship rowing medals. The other function of the Club is to organise rowing within the university, which at any one time may involve a quarter of the university population. This culminates in the Bumping Races held at the end of the Trinity term. Today there is a host of boat clubs belonging to the various colleges along the banks of the River Thames, along with the City of Oxford Rowing Club building further along by Donnington Bridge.

[Aerial view of the Oxford boathouses – Donnington Bridge and the City of Oxford Rowing Club are around half a mile further along the River Thames to the right of the picture]

The University Boat House (now destroyed by fire) was used in filming *The Secret of Bay 5B* along with the City of Oxford Rowing Club where the arrest of Edward Manley is made. In *The Daughters of Cain* Ted Brooks' body is found by a college boatman close to Donnington Bridge. The boathouses used in filming *Lewis: Reputation* were those of Corpus Christi and St. John's College as well as shots along the towpath opposite. Most recently University College boathouse was used in *Lewis: Old, Unhappy, Far Off Things*, and again in *Lewis: Generation of Vipers*.

BODLEIAN LIBRARY

Opened in 1602 the Bodleian Library is one of the oldest libraries in Europe, though not the first university library in Oxford. That was

15

situated in a room above the congregation house at the church of St. Mary the Virgin, and contained books donated by Thomas Cobham, (Bishop of Worcester) between 1317 and 1327. The books were dispersed after his death to pay for his debts and funeral expenses, but later redeemed and deposited in Oriel College. Around 1337 the Commissary of the University declared the library the property of the University of Oxford and had the books moved back to St. Mary's.

[Entrance to the Divinity School]

Other books followed from the library of Humfrey (Duke of Gloucester and younger brother of Henry V) to the extent that the room was not large enough. The collection was to be moved to the Divinity School, then under construction, but this was not to be complete until 1489, more than forty years after Humfrey's death in 1447. It was called the Duke Humfrey's Library and has an elaborate ceiling with arms of the University in the panels and the arms of Thomas Bodley at the intersections.

By the middle of the 16th century the University was in financial crisis, and according to Sir Thomas Bodley the Library 'in every part' lay 'in ruined and waste'. Much of the collection had also been dispersed, and it was Bodley who offered to bring the Library back to 'its proper use, and to make it fitte, and handsome with seates, and shelves and Deskes'. The building was refitted and restocked with books at the expense of Bodley, and other benefactors, and reopened on 8th November 1602.

In 1610 Bodley came to an agreement with the Stationers' Company, which undertook to send a copy of every book registered at Stationers' Hall to the Library. As might be imagined, the number of books in the Library increased dramatically, though Bodley did not accept everything sent to him since he considered many volumes to be 'idle bookes, & riffe raffes' which ought never to 'com into the Librarie'. Due to his own biases there was a poor representation of English literature and a complete absence of early editions of Jacobean dramatists for many years.

[Inside the Bodleian Library (date unknown)]

Soon extensions to the Library were needed. The first was built over the Divinity School, between 1610 and 1612, and became known as the Arts End. The ceiling was painted with numerous coats of arms and the folios were chained to the lower shelves. Next the two-storey quadrangle, used for lectures, was rebuilt and a third storey for storage was added in 1624. This is the Schools Quadrangle. The old building was extended in the same style as the Arts End and became known as the Selden End, after John Selden, who gave eight thousand volumes to the Library along with a collection of oriental manuscripts. On the second floor is a frieze of some two hundred famous men painted around 1620. Books continued to flood in from numerous benefactors including Alexander Pope, Benjamin Franklin and Samuel Johnson, to the extent that by 1861 the library once more needed to expand – which it did by taking over the Radcliffe Camera.

However, space still needed to be found and in 1939, thanks mainly to a large donation by the Rockefeller Foundation, the New Bodleian Library was completed. It should also be mentioned that Kenneth Grahame made the Bodleian Library his heir and bequeathed the income resulting from the copyright of *The Wind in the Willows* in addition to the original holograph manuscript. Today the library has absorbed those of the Radcliffe Science Library, the Indian Institute, Rhodes House, the Law Library and the John Johnson Collection. It has around eleven million books on over one hundred miles of shelving and is, as ever, in need of further room to expand.

The Bodleian Library featured in the very first Inspector Morse episode, *The Dead of Jericho*. Its next appearance was in *The Settling of the Sun* (in which Morse walks past the statue of the 3rd Earl of Pembroke and out of the main gate, holding the exhibition programme *Images of Christ: Giotto – Dali* that shows a stigmata.

Its most notable, if not infamous, appearance in *Inspector Morse* is as the location for the shooting from a library window of Welsh diva, Gwladys Probert, in *Twilight of the Gods*. A revolver is later found behind the some books in the library.

Finally when Morse is ill in hospital with a perforated ulcer (*The Wench is Dead*), he begins to investigate a historical murder mystery: the murder of Joanna Franks on the Oxford canal in 1859. A fellow patient's daughter, Christine Greenaway, works at the Bodleian Library and agrees to lend her librarian skills to the case. In this episode Dr. Van Buren is seen walking across Schools Quadrangle and into the Library where she sees Kershaw in a reading room.

In *Lewis: Whom the Gods Would Destroy* Lewis and Hathaway seek out Professor Gold in Seymour College Library and ask her about Greely's notes in Greek. This was filmed in Duke Humfrey's Library while at the very end of the episode the three again meet up in the Bodleian Library with the film credits about to roll as Lewis walks off in the direction of Broad Street. A body is found among the basement stacks in *Lewis: And the Moonbeams Kiss the Sea* which also used the maintenance room for the filming.

BOTANIC GARDENS

[The botanic gardens with Magdalen tower in the background]

In 1621 the Oxford Physic Garden was established by Henry Danvers (Earl of Danby) and is, surely the oldest such garden after those of Pisa and Leyden. The objective was to use the garden for 'the advancement of the faculty of medicine' but in fact it was used for botany, medicine and practical gardening from the start. In 1840 it was renamed the Botanic Garden and today it boasts an alpine garden, a fernery, a grass garden, herbaceous borders, a water garden and a collection of historical roses. In the greenhouses are tropical plants, including bananas and rice, collections of ferns, succulents, orchids, insect-eating plants and water lilies. Notable firsts for the garden were the production of its own weed, the Oxford ragwort (*Senecio squalidus*) and the London plane (a hybrid of an oriental and American species raised in 1665).

[The Inigo Jones gate at the botanic gardens (date unknown)]

Danby had originally leased five acres of land from Magdalen College for his garden, which had formally been a Jewish burial ground. First the ground had to be raised above the River Cherwell flood plain, which took four thousand loads of 'mucke and dunge'. The gateway was built by Inigo Jones's master mason, Nicholas Stone, in 1632. An innkeeper, Jacob Bobart, who was also a competent gardener, became the first Keeper in 1642. The job had been offered to John Tradescant, most associated with the Ashmolean Museum, who due to failing health had been unable to accept the post. Bobart was a good choice and produced the first catalogue of plants in 1648, by which time there were one thousand six hundred specimens. The formal design of the garden was by Robert Morison, first Professor of Botany in Oxford, who had been superintendent of the Duke of Orlean's famous garden at Blois.

Bobart's son succeeded his father as Keeper, and after Morison's death became Professor of Botany as well. It was Professor Daubeny, appointed in 1834, who changed the name of the garden and was the first to use it for experimental research. He also gave a party there for the victorious Darwinians after the famous debate between Huxley and Wilberforce, over which he had presided at the Oxford British Association meeting in 1860. A garden outside the entrance, designed by Sylvia Crowe, now commemorates Oxford's wartime contribution to the science of antibiotics through the development of penicillin.

The Botanic Gardens feature in the opening scenes of *The Settling of the Sun* when the Reverend Robson fatally collapses after awful memories of wartime Japan are brought back to his troubled mind. Also in *The Silent World of Nicholas Quinn* Lewis catches up with Roope as he frames Bartlett here, and there is a passing shot in *Death is now My Neighbour*. In *Deceived by Flight* Morse and Anthony Donn eat their fish and chips in the gardens, with Magdalen Bridge in the background, while talking about Zen and one hand clapping.

In *Lewis: Reputation* Lewis is seen running through the gardens, while in *Lewis: Old School Ties* Stephen, Caroline, David and Jo have a picnic and go punting along the riverbank close to the Botanic Gardens. This picturesque location returns for appearances in *Lewis: Life Born of Fire* as where Jonjo Read goes jogging and Lewis and Zoe Kenneth talk, while in *Lewis: Music to Die For* some of the dramatic river scenes were filmed here, although the climax at the lock is actually Bowers Lock on the River Wey in Guildford, Surrey. Its most prominent use to date has been in *Lewis: The Soul of Genius*, with the murder taking place here.

BRASENOSE COLLEGE

[Brasenose College from Radcliffe Square]

The College takes its name from the bronze sanctuary knocker, first recorded in a document of 1279, which used to be attached to the main gate of the Brasenose Hall. The importance of the knocker was that colleges, like churches, were regarded as sanctuaries and so any fugitives were safe from the authorities once they had clutched the knocker. It was removed to Stamford in the 1330s, since Oxford was considered at that time to be too turbulent a place. In 1890 it was brought back to Oxford and has hung ever since in the hall, over high table. Over the centuries many halls have occupied the site which today is Brasenose College. These included Burwaldescote (1247-1469), Amsterdam, St. Thomas's Hall (formerly Staple Hall), Sheld Hall, Ivy Hall, Little University Hall, Salysbury Hall and Little Edmund Hall.

Brasenose College was founded in 1509 by William Smyth, Bishop of Lincoln, and Richard Sutton, a successful lawyer. Since at this time the original knocker was at Stamford a new brazen nose was produced which contains the caricature of a human face. This knocker is presently located at the apex of the main gate, while stained-glass representations may be found in the northern oriel window in the hall, alongside portraits of the two founders. The college coat of arms consists of devices of the founders and the diocese of Lincoln, and is one of only three known examples of tierced arms in England, the others belonging to Lincoln and Corpus Christi Colleges.

The college prospered due to the generosity of the early benefactors, though there was discontent among the Junior Fellows, who considered their income too low in comparison to the Senior Fellows and the Principal. It was not without financial scandal, to the extent that in 1643 some Fellows petitioned King Charles I to institute a Visitation. Most of these abuses flourished under the autocratic rule of Principal Radcliffe (1614-48). However, despite these setbacks the college expanded to twenty-one Fellows from the original twelve. Probably the most famous Principal of the 16th century was Alexander Nowell, who is also credited with the invention of bottled beer.

After the Civil War in 1647 the College was in debt again and experienced a Parliamentary Visitation. Principal Radcliffe was ousted and Daniel Greenwood intruded in his place. He was largely responsible for turning the college finances around and ensuring the stability of Brasenose for the next century, during which time the college became firmly Jacobite. Whereas the 18th century saw Brasenose as a place of intellectual distinction the 19th century saw it acquire a new reputation for sporting achievements, particularly in rowing and cricket.

Among the notables of Brasenose College are Sir Charles Holmes (director of the National Gallery from 1916-28), John Buchan, Field-

Marshall Earl Haig, Lord Scarman, Robert Runcie (former Archbishop of Canterbury) and John Mortimer. Today the College has forty Fellows, twenty-three lecturers, ninety-two graduates and three hundred and twenty-nine undergraduates. Since 1974 it has been co-residential. In architecture the building is a curious amalgam of Gothic and Baroque. For instance, on the parapet there is an odd mixture of Baroque urns and Gothic pinnacles.

Brasenose College is the Lonsdale College of the Inspector Morse novels and also in the television adaptations. In *The Dead of Jericho*, Catherine Edgeley was an undergraduate here, while in *The Way Through the Woods* Dr. Alan Hardinge lectured and had rooms in the college. In *The Riddle of the Third Mile*, the plot is based around the contest for the Master of Lonsdale, and Morse is invited to a supper there to celebrate the election of the successful candidate.

[The knocker above the entrance (left) and sundial on north side of the Old Quadrangle (right) are the two most famous icons at Brasenose College]

As for film credits, the college was featured in *The Silent World of Nicholas Quinn* where Roope was interviewed in his room in New Quadrangle, and again in *The Settling of the Sun* where the reception dinner (at which Morse is a guest) is interrupted by the murder of a Japanese student. In *The Last Enemy* the college changes its name to Beaumont College while in *Twilight of the Gods* it is where Sir John Gielgud, as Chancellor, rehearses his speech about other places called Oxford. Its other lesser appearances (which are usually characterised by having the giant sundial dating from 1719 in shot) are in *The Last Enemy*, *The Way Through the Woods*, *The Daughters of Cain* and finally in

Death is now My Neighbour. Brasenose Lane adjacent to the college is where Lewis can be seen walking while removing his bow tie after the concert in *Lewis: Whom the Gods Would Destroy*, and was again used in *Lewis: Falling Darkness.* Brasenose College is also Mayfield College in *Lewis: Life Born of Fire* (although some of the scenes were also shot at Lincoln College), and most recently it has appeared in *Lewis: Counter Culture Blues* and *Lewis: The Dead of Winter.*

BRIDGE OF SIGHS

The Bridge of Sighs as it is known to almost all, due to a misconception that it resembles the bridge of the same name in Venice, though it actually more closely resembles the nearby and much larger Rialto Bridge in construction, is in fact Hertford Bridge, built by Sir Thomas Jackson in 1913-14, to simply link the two parts of Hertford College. There is an old (untrue) story that, due to the bridge being in place, Hertford College students became the heaviest in Oxford and consequently the authorities closed the bridge in order to give the students more exercise.

[Hertford Bridge, quite a tricky place to drive a bus under!]

It is, however, a distinctive city landmark at the bottom end of Broad Street, over New College Lane, which today is a dead end, although in

1965 it seems that this was a major thoroughfare since the bus carrying a young Morse passes under the bridge at the beginning of *Endeavour: First Bus to Woodstock*. The keen observer will also be able to spot this location in the background in any number of other *Inspector Morse* and *Lewis* episodes most notably *The Dead of Jericho, The Last Bus to Woodstock, Death is now my Neighbour, Lewis: Generation of Vipers* and no less than three times in *Lewis: The Indelible Stain*, while the college itself was featured in *The Last Bus to Woodstock, The Ghost in the Machine, Dead on Time* and *Lewis: The Great and the Good*.

CARFAX

Carfax is the ancient heart of Oxford where the four roads from the North, South, West and East Gates of the city met. It was also the highest point of the old city and derives its name from the Latin *quadrifurcus* meaning four-forked. Cattle were slaughtered here in the 13th century, and in 1610 the Carfax Conduit was erected to receive piped spring water from Hinksey Hill. It was removed to Nuneham Park in 1789 due to the Oxford Mileways Act of 1771, which resulted in street widening and other improvements. Other features of Carfax were the City Church of St. Martin, the Synndal Tavern, Butter Bench and Penniless Bench (the semi-official meeting place of the City Council where members would gather at the ringing of the bell of St. Martin's and wait until the coming of the Mayor).

[The clock and bells on the east side of Carfax tower]

Penniless Bench had already been removed by 1789, and all but the tower of St. Martin's was demolished due to further street widening under the Oxford Corporation Act of 1890. The tower was restored in 1897 and today provides excellent views of the city. The 17th century clock and replicas of the two quarter-boys (figures of men holding clubs in quaint Roman costumes with gold helmets) were moved to the east side of the tower in 1898 and fitted with two quarter-jack bells. Below is the city's motto *Fortis est Veritas*.

In *The Secret of Annexe 3* Margaret Bowman visits Carfax tower with unknown intentions and remembers a scare at a school visit to Snowdon before realising the tower is shut for the winter months. Meanwhile in *Death is now My Neighbour*, Morse catches a bus to Carfax to get a haircut and to show his barber a photograph that is important to the case. Does Morse always need more than one reason to do something? It appears on film in *The Last Enemy* as Morse discards his newspaper as he passes the tower on his way to Beaumont College. There are also passing shots in *Death is now My Neighbour* and *Greeks Bearing Gifts*.

Its most remembered image though is that of the drunk by the tower in *Happy Families* – who is actually Colin Dexter making his usual cameo appearance.

CHERWELL BOAT HOUSE

[A quiet place for a fish & chip supper]

In 1901 a lease was taken from St. John's College for a landing stage for punts on the Upper River Cherwell beyond Bardwell Road. By 1904 the Cherwell Boat House had been built, and by 1909 a separate residence, now the Cherwell Boathouse Restaurant, was also in evidence. Being a little off the tourist track this stretch of the river was used mainly by residents.

In 1964 the concern was purchased by Lieutenant-Commander Perowne (Retired) and it was he who set about establishing the restaurant, which was subsequently sold in 1968 to a science graduate named Anthony Verdin. In addition the latter re-established the business of boat-building and is the only punt-builder in Oxford. The business expanded when in 1984 a new building, complete with roof terrace, was erected for housing the seventy plus punts in regular use. It site is still owned and run by the Verdin family today.

Although Inspector Morse never visited, it has become a favourite for Inspector Lewis, no doubt helped by the fact that it is in a quiet location at the end of a lane – ideal for film crews. It first appeared in *Lewis: The Point of Vanishing* and again in *Lewis: The Mind Has Mountains*, with the final and most memorable appearance being in *Lewis: Your Sudden Death Question* when at the end of the episode Lewis finds that the restaurant is fully booked and so resorts to having a romantic fish and chip supper with Laura Hobson by the candle lit punts.

CHRIST CHURCH COLLEGE & MEADOW

Christ Church was the thirteenth Oxford college to be built and remains one of the largest, though its foundation was a complex process. Originally the site was occupied by the Augustinian Saint Frideswide's Priory which was dissolved in 1524 during the reign of King Henry VIII. At that time the area around the priory was occupied by houses, a hospital, churches, the Oxford Jewry and Canterbury College (the home of the monks of Christ Church, Canterbury). Under the direction of Cardinal Wolsey demolition began in 1525 but the priory church was largely unaffected save for the westernmost bays being destroyed, since the remainder of the building was to be incorporated into the new Cardinal College. By the time of Wolsey's fall from power in 1529 three sides of the Great Quadrangle were virtually complete, although only the foundations of the planned chapel were in place. The hall and kitchen were completed in 1529 and have remained intact ever since. King Henry VIII took over the fabric and endowments of

27

Wolsey's foundation and renamed it King Henry VIII's College. This only lasted until 1546 when he designated the former priory church as Christ Church Cathedral of the new Henrician diocese of Oxford and as the chapel to the new college of Christ Church.

[Tom Tower, one of the entrances to Christ Church College]

Major additions have been made to the buildings through the centuries, and Wolsey's Great Quadrangle was crowned with a gate-tower designed by Sir Christopher Wren. To this day the bell in the gate-tower, Great Tom, is rung one hundred and one times every night at nine o'clock Oxford time (which is five minutes behind that of Greenwich) in honour of the hundred original scholars of the college plus the one added in 1664. In former times this also signalled the closing of all college gates throughout Oxford.

The Great Hall was the work of two of the greatest craftsmen of their time: the mason Thomas Redman and the glazier James Nicholson. It is reached via a wide stairway enhanced by the most delicate fan tracery dating from around 1640, although the current stairs only date from 1805. The Great Hall itself is dominated by the large hammerbeam roof, richly carved and gilded. Among the notable portraits upon its panelled walls are those of Lewis Carroll and John Wesley. It is interesting to note that King Charles I held his Parliament here during the English Civil War.

[The Great Hall is recognisable to any Harry Potter enthusiasts]

Christ Church has produced many famous people, including thirteen British prime ministers (the two most recent being Anthony Eden, 1955-1957 and Sir Alec Douglas-Home, 1963–1964), which is more than all the other Oxford colleges put together, and more than any Cambridge college (and two short of the total number for the University of Cambridge). Even Albert Einstein had a five year research studentship here from 1931.

The college is the setting for parts of Evelyn Waugh's *Brideshead Revisited*, as well as being an inspiration for Lewis Carroll's *Alice's Adventures in Wonderland*. More recently it has been used in the filming of Philip Pullman's *The Golden Compass*, and perhaps most notably has featured in the Harry Potter series as Hogwarts (although the Great Hall was deemed too small, for filming, with a replica one and a half times the size being built in the studio). In *Twilight of the Gods* the drinks party with John Gielgud is held in Tom Quad after the ceremony, while in *The Daughters of Cain* Morse interviews Brownlee here. In *Lewis: The Indelible Stain* the American academic, Paul Yelland, who is accused of racism, appears to be helped from the college (which is supposed to be the Oxford Union) across the road to his lodgings at Pembroke College where he is later found murdered

Just to the south of the college is Christ Church Meadow which runs behind the Faculty of Music and police station. It is still grazed upon by cattle and in 1346 was said to be forty-six acres in size. In fact part of the land was a gift by Lady Montacute to maintain her chantry in the Lady Chapel in the original priory. The tourist should beware since there are restrictions to entry, outlined on the notice board in Rose Lane:

> The Meadow Keepers and Constables are hereby instructed to prevent the entrance into the Meadow of all beggars, all persons in ragged or very dirty clothes, persons of improper character or who are not decent in appearance and behaviour; and to prevent indecent, rude or disorderly conduct of every description.

The meadow has been used as a backdrop several times in filming and is most easily recognised in *The Secret of Bay 5B*, *Twilight of the Gods*, *Lewis: Old, Unhappy, Far Off Things* and finally in *Lewis: The Indelible Stain* in which Lewis and Hathaway walk along Broad Walk. Other college appearances are in *Last Seen Wearing*, *The Day of the Devil* and *Deadly Slumber*.

COVERED MARKET

The covered market dates back as far as 1771 when John Gwynn showed his draft plans for such a market to provide for meat, fish, poultry, vegetables and herbs, to replace the existing street markets in Fish Street (St. Aldate's) and Butcher Row (Queen Street). The cost of construction was estimated at £5,647.

[The covered market with the post box marking the centre]

The market, costing considerably less due to sale of surplus property, opened on 1st November 1774 and consisted of twenty butchers' shops, which opened every day but were supplemented three days a week by country butchers who were also allowed to sell their wares. Within a year eight further shops and forty stalls selling all manner of goods were in operation. The shops were divided into blocks by wide avenues, with everything being supervised by a beadle. The market was so successful it soon needed to expand, but this was not to happen until the 1830s when Thomas Wyatt the younger had the market extended beneath an iron roof. Further extensive reconstructions took place in the 1880s and 1890s. Today the market is little changed, maintaining much of its Victorian atmosphere, and flourishes with a good mix of all the original trades plus many boutique and specialist establishments.

In *Absolute Conviction* Charlie Bennett is chased by Morse and Lewis, with the former falling over a greengrocery stall in the market, so ending the chase. The market also appears in *Greeks Bearing Gifts* where it helps Maria (the dead man's sister) evade Jocasta (the interpreter). More recently it has made an appearance in *Lewis: Counter Culture Blues, Lewis: Falling Darkness* and *Lewis: The Soul of Genius.*

EAGLE & CHILD PUBLIC HOUSE

Situated at No. 49 St. Giles', the Eagle and Child has been an inn since 1650 and is named after the family of the Earl of Derby, whose crest was a coronet with eagle and child. The tavern was a favourite haunt of the diarist Anthony Wood in the 17th century and of the group of friends, centred on C. S. Lewis, known as the Inklings. They met to drink, talk and read aloud their compositions.

[The *Bird and Baby* public house]

Their members included J. R. R. Tolkien, Charles Williams, Nevill Coghill and H. V. D. Dyson. The public house is known locally as the *Bird and Baby*.

The Secret of Annexe 3 finds Morse and Lewis in the Eagle and Child, taking their "lunchtime calories". Lewis reads the plaque commemorating the fact that C. S. Lewis, W. H. Lewis, J. R. R. Tolkien and Charles Williams met there for many years, each Tuesday, to drink and talk about literary endeavours and other subjects. The alcohol gets him wondering whether another plaque will describe how he and Morse sat there to solve this bizarre puzzle.

On film this public house can be seen in *Second Time Around* and *The Way Through the Woods*. More recently in *Lewis: Allegory of Love* the Inklings reform here with Dorian Crane being murdered soon afterwards with a sword, but although the exterior shots were correct the interior was actually The Dove public house in Hammersmith, London.

EASTGATE HOTEL

[The location of Lewis's flat?]

The site at No. 73 High Street was originally occupied by an inn called the Cross and Sword – which dated from at least 1605. It was demolished in 1772 and around 1840 another inn, the Flying Horse, was built on the same site. The current hotel, whose entrance is in Merton Street, takes its name from the east gate to the old city that stood in Merton Street. It was designed by E. P. Warren and completed in 1900 with an enlargement in 1964-65.

Although not a major location it does have a Lewis claim to fame as in the early *Lewis* episodes this appears to be where Lewis has his flat since, he is seen emerging from here in *Lewis: The Great and the Good*, and the hotel was used again in *Lewis: The Mind Has Mountains*. This is further evidenced when Lewis, helped by Hathaway, disposes of an old mattress in somebody else's skip just around the corner in Merton Street. However, Lewis seems to have moved out of Oxford more recently, for the current filming location for his flat is in Twickenham.

EXAMINATION SCHOOLS

[It is here that all examination results are displayed]

It may come as a surprise, but initially examinations were not a large part of any of the Oxford colleges. It was only the examination statutes of 1849 and 1850 that produced a demand for increased accommodation for written examinations, which up to that point had all taken place under the auspices of the Bodleian Library – who were by now in need of more space for the ever-increasing book collections.

Although the committee of 1859 recommended the building of 'new examination schools' it was some twenty years before this was put into effect. Indeed there was much arguing, and no less than three architectural competitions held with the winner being Thomas Graham Jackson, who proposed a building in the High Street on the site of the old

Angel Inn. The building was completed and handed over to the Vice-Chancellor on the 13ᵗʰ May 1882, with the first examinations taking place six days later.

The building is a mixture of Elizabethan and Jacobean country house styles with a quadrangle and tower resembling the one in the Old Schools Quadrangle. The Great Hall is strikingly lofty with a hammerbeam roof and a floor of variously coloured marbles forming mosaics. The upper floor has marble columns and opens into two large 'writing schools' intended for two hundred candidates each, while on the next level there is a third room for one hundred and twenty candidates.

The final cost of £180,000 (including interest charges) stretched the University's finances to the limit, with the colleges making no contribution. Indeed it was only in 1909, thanks to a private benefactor, that the carving in the Great Hall was completed, and 1978 that a clock was to adorn the tower. During both World Wars the building became a military hospital.

Although never featured in *Inspector Morse* the examination halls have appeared twice in *Lewis*. In *Lewis: Music to Die For* they became the Oxford University Boxing Club, while in *Lewis: The Dead of Winter* they rather strangely double for the exterior of Brasenose College.

EXETER COLLEGE

Walter de Stapledon (Bishop of Exeter and Treasurer to Edward II) was the founder of the Exeter College in 1314, though at that time it was known as Stapledon Hall. It was mainly a place for the education of prospective parish clergy and as such was one of the poorest of Oxford establishments and often in debt. In fact the only income was from tithes of the Cornish church of Gwinear, and those from Long Wittenham in Berkshire, along with some Oxford property that in total amounted to not much more than £50 per annum in 1355. Originally there were only thirteen Fellows, including the Rector and Chaplain, and the statutes stated that all of these with the exception of the Chaplain were to come from the diocese of Exeter and to study philosophy. There was no provision for the study of theology and the maximum term of stay was thirteen years (comparatively short for those times). In 1405 the name was changed to Exeter College and by now more buildings had been added – St. Stephen's Hall, a chapel, a library and what was known as Palmer's tower.

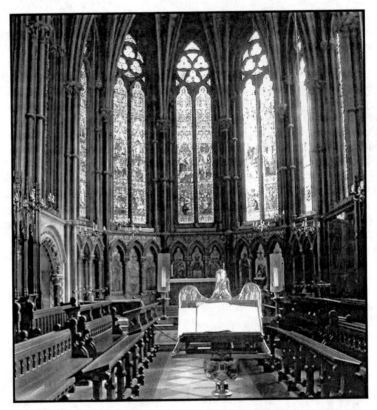

[Inside the chapel at Exeter College]

Fortunes were to change when William Petre, a former undergraduate of the college, became both powerful and wealthy and on retirement in 1566 devoted some time to reorganising the place. He endowed seven new Fellowships that were now widened to include people from Devon, Somerset, Dorset, Oxfordshire and Essex. He gave four Oxford rectories (Kidlington, Merton, South Newington and Yarnton) which provided financial stability, and made the Fellows' appointments for life. By the early 17th century the college had become a fashionable place for lawyers and politicians as well as the clergy, but all was to change again during the English Civil War when King Charles I took much of the valuable silver for his own use.

It was not until the Victorian era that the college once again prospered, with Fellowships not being restricted by geography, and much building work taking place, with Sir George Gilbert Scott, who was also the architect behind the Martyrs' Memorial, being responsible for the present chapel, library, Rector's lodgings, Broad Street gateway and tower, and the range running west from the tower. The style was most certainly Gothic.

Among the famous who studied here are William Morris (artist), Charles Lyell (father of modern geology), R. D. Blackmore (author), J. R. R. Tolkien (author), Richard Burton (actor), Alan Bennett (playwright), Sir Roger Bannister (athlete) and even Ralph Sherwin who was executed for his faith in 1581 and was later canonised by Pope Paul VI in 1970 and thus becomes the only Fellow of the college to become a saint.

The college is used in a number of scenes in *The Settling of the Sun*. An Oxford summer school brings together both students and college staff who have past dark secrets and scores to settle. Inspector Morse unwittingly provides an alibi as he awards a crossword prize at the welcoming dinner, and must see through a number of disguises and hidden motives before the heart of the matter is revealed. It is also the college through which Lewis chases Roope in *The Silent World of Nicholas Quinn*. Scenes in *Happy Families* and *The Way Through the Woods* were also shot here. Rather strangely in *Lewis: Expiation* the exterior of Merton College is shown while the interior shots are definitely of Exeter College. It also appeared in *Lewis: Life Born of Fire* as the location for McKewan's room, while the grounds were where the open air play, *The Merchant of Venice*, was taking place in *Lewis: The Quality of Mercy* (filming which incidentally took no less than eight full days to complete in August 2008). In 2011 more extensive filming was done as the place became Carlisle College in *Lewis: The Soul of Genius*.

Most notably though it is the setting in *The Remorseful Day* where Inspector Morse having just listened to *In Paradisum* in the college Chapel collapses on the lawn outside. From here he is taken to the John Radcliffe Hospital where he subsequently dies.

HOLYWELL MUSIC ROOM

The Holywell Music Room is the oldest reputed surviving concert hall in the world. It all started in 1742 when a subscription was started, probably by William Hayes, the Professor of Music. The design of the sixty-five by thirty-two foot building was by Thomas Camplin, though due to lack of funds completion was not until 1748, after which time concerts continued until 1838 (with only a brief pause between 1789 and 1793).

Thereafter its use was widened and included among its activities auctions and lectures. In 1901 the Oxford University Musical Society purchased the lease, after which time it reverted to purely musical use. Now administered by the Faculty of Music it is used for numerous small-scale musical events for up to 250 people. A new chamber organ was installed in 1985. Today it is famous for its regular Sunday morning Coffee Concerts.

[The Holywell Music Room]

In *Inspector Morse* terms it will always be the place where Gwladys Probert gave her master class shortly before her death in *Twilight of the Gods*. It was also where Morse consulted Ian Matthews about the forged Whistler painting, and later the Dürer picture of Giovanni Bellini in *Who Killed Harry Field?* The Holywell Music Room also became the Dimittus offices in *Lewis: Music to Die For*. Almost adjacent at No. 99 Holywell Street is the location of Fiona McKendrick's house in *Lewis: The Point of Vanishing*.

JERICHO

Jericho was Oxford's first suburb, lying in the ancient Walton Manor to the northwest of the city wall in old Northgate Hundred — an area uninhabited until the 19th century. The name, often used to signify remoteness, is popularly thought to have its origin in the jerry-builders who constructed it, though it was actually taken from Jericho Gardens, which lay to the west of the Radcliffe Infirmary when the hospital opened in 1770. The gardens were mentioned as early as 1688 by Anthony Wood, when there was also an inn named Jericho close to the present location of Jericho House.

[Oxford University Press Building in Jericho (date unknown)]

Jericho was an area of commercial importance due to the Oxford Canal which was completed in 1790 (connecting the Rivers Trent and Mersey) and passes through this suburb. In 1825 the Jericho Iron and Brass Foundry was built. This is a working-class and student quarter which is also the home of the new Oxford University Press building constructed between 1826 and 1832. The streets are laid out on a simple grid pattern bounded by St. Sepulchre's cemetery to the north, Walton Street to the east, Worcester College to the south and the canal to the west. As with many such areas Jericho saw cholera epidemics, particularly in 1832, 1849 and 1854.

In Victorian times Jericho became the centre of the Oxford Movement. Local religion centred on Thomas Coombe, superintendent of the Clarendon Press, who made provision for schools and the building of St. Barnabas Church in Canal Street.

[Scene of Morse's first on screen drink (top) and murder (bottom)]

The Bookbinder's Arms (now the Old Bookbinders) is featured several times in both the original novel and the television adaptation of *The Dead of Jericho*. In the novel the public house is known as the Printers Devil. In both versions the public house is opposite to the entrance to Canal Reach (Canal Street) where Anne Scott (Staveley in the television adaptation) and George Jackson, both victims of the Jericho killings, lived. It might interest the reader to know that currently (2012) the end house on the right in Coombe Road used in filming *The Dead of Jericho* is up for sale. The asking price for this two-bedroom house is £400,000.

In the novel, Morse, quite naturally, enjoys a couple of double Scotches here. George Jackson made a short visit there, enjoying the one armed bandit before returning home for the last time. In the finale it provides the setting for Lewis to give Morse two poignant letters from Anne Scott, one for Morse himself, and another for her lover, Charles Richards.

In the television adaptation, Morse has to explain in the public house why he has just secretly entered Anne Staveley's house. Morse and Lewis return there to celebrate Lewis's birthday and for Morse to expound his theories based upon the Greek tragedy, *Oedipus Rex* by Sophocles.

[The scene of the fire where Hathaway is saved by Lewis]

The southern end of Canal Street comes to a junction with Wellington Street and Nelson Street. It was on this apex at No. 31 that the climax of *Lewis: Life Born of Fire* was filmed. This scene involved Lewis having to save a drugged Hathaway from inside the now burning house. All is quickly put in order though, for in the opening title sequence of the very next episode *Lewis: The Great and the Good* the viewer sees the junction from above with no sign of any fire damage. In the same episode No. 54 Nelson Street was also used as Cooper's flat.

Also worthy of note is the Phoenix cinema (then Studio 2) in Walton Street, Jericho, which was showing *The Last Tango In Paris* from which Bartlett is seen exiting in *The Silent World of Nicholas Quinn*. Morse and Lewis later return to check on his ticket stub that is central to Bartlett's alibi. Morse and Lewis also return at the very end of the episode only to find that the film has been changed to a Disney classic, which delights Lewis who goes home to fetch his wife and children while Morse consoles himself by going to the public house adjacent to the cinema. Finally Le Petit Blanc restaurant in Walton Street was where Geoffrey Owens takes his girlfriend for lunch in *Death is now My Neighbour*.

KING'S ARMS PUBLIC HOUSE

[Looking down on the King's Arms from the Sheldonian Theatre]

Buildings were first erected at No. 40 Holywell Street in 1268 by the Augustinian Friars who owned the site until 1540. On 18th September 1607 they became the King's Arms public house (in honour of King James I) and contained many lodging rooms, a large stable and back courtyard. It soon became a popular place for plays, and although parts of the original inn still remain, in the early 18th century the south frontage and rear wing were rebuilt, with a staircase and a stone oak-beamed cellar being added. The west front was added in the late 18th century, and by 1771 this public house had become a coaching inn on the London to Gloucester run. Wadham College converted the upper floors into student's rooms in 1962.

It is here that Rosemary Henderson sits and is chased out by Morse and also where later Morse and Lewis meet in *The Secret of Bay 5B*, while in *Deadly Slumber* John Brewster's girlfriend, Jane Folley, follows him from here in an attempt to persuade him to come out. This public house also appears prominently, albeit now as The Grapevine, in *Lewis: Allegory of Love*.

LADY MARGARET HALL

[The pristine red brick of Lady Margaret Hall]

Lady Margaret Hall was founded in 1878 as a 'small hall or hostel in connection with the Church of England for the reception of women desirous of availing themselves of the special advantages which Oxford offers for higher education'. The name is taken from Lady Margaret Beaufort, the mother of King Henry VII and a patron of learning.

The original building was a villa constructed in grey brick that soon became too small, the more dominant red brick structures being added in 1881 and 1884 respectively. It is interesting to note that the land was actually leased from St. John's College who stipulated that the buildings should be of a simple design that could be converted into ordinary housing should the idea of a women's college not prove a success (and it should be remembered that women were not admitted to the University formally until 1920). Other buildings have been added over the years as the college expanded and acquired the freehold for the original site in 1923.

The college is not in the centre of Oxford, being situated in a quiet residential area off the Banbury Road, but it does have the advantage of a large sweep of land along the River Cherwell. This also makes it ideal for filming and although *Inspector Morse* was never shot here it has been utilised in the *Lewis* series when in *Lewis: Old, Unhappy, Far Off Things* it was the natural choice to be Lady Matilda's College, with no less than eight full days of filming taking place here during November 2010.

LAMB & FLAG PUBLIC HOUSE

[Lamb & Flag in St. Giles']

Originally owned by Godstow Abbey it was purchased by St. John's College along with the rest of St. Giles' around 1695 when it was just known as The Lamb (the current name referring to the symbol for St. John the Baptist). Much of the original building remains with clinker rooms and uneven floors adding to the atmosphere to the place, The main bar is adorned by heraldic crests of every college in Oxford. The one Inspector Morse association is that this is where a young Morse takes a drink and apologises to Rosalind Stromming in *Endeavour: First Bus to Woodstock.*

LINCOLN COLLEGE

The College of the Blessed Mary and All Saints, Lincoln in the University of Oxford (to give the college its full title) was founded on 13th October 1427 by Richard Fleming, the then Bishop of Lincoln and is one of the older colleges in the city. He intended it to be 'a little college' with the aim of training the clergy 'in true theology' so that they could 'defend the mysteries of Scripture against those ignorant laymen who profaned with swinish snouts its most holy pearls'. To this effect, he obtained a charter for the college from King Henry VI, which combined the parishes of All Saints, St. Michael's at the North Gate and St. Mildred's (which was immediately demolished) within the college under a rector, and hence provided revenue, albeit small in comparison with other Oxford colleges, to pay stipends for the chaplains to the churches.

[The 'dreaming spire' of the library]

The college for much of its history was impoverished but one highlight was the library (now with 60,000 volumes housed in the old church of All Saints after a transformation by Robert Potter in 1971-5). Between 1465 and 1474 Robert Fleming (Dean of Lincoln) gave a rich collection of manuscripts that were added to the already useful collection of scholastic theology books.

Today the upper reading room, or Cohen Room, has an elaborate plastered ceiling, and the Senior Library (downstairs) holds some of the college's older books.

These include pamphlets from the English Civil War period, Wesleyana, and plays dating from the late 17th and early 18th centuries, as well as a small collection of manuscripts. The science library is also to be found downstairs.

The college did expand slowly, due to benefactors such as the Bishop of Rotherham, who brought into the college's possession the Bicester Inn (now the Mitre Hotel), while Bishop William Smyth of Lincoln gave the college the manor of Bushbury in Wolverhampton. In 1608-9 through the beneficence of Sir Thomas Rotheram the west range of the chapel quadrangle was built, which was followed in 1629-31 by the east range and the chapel itself. In 1640 a new cellar was excavated under the hall, and a ball court and bowling green created. Just as the college fortunes seemed to be secure the Civil War broke out with the consequence that the college silver went to swell the royal mint, and when the Parliamentarians won, the loyalist Fellows were all expelled and replaced by nominees chosen by the parliamentary regime (five of them were later deprived of their position after the Restoration in 1660). The college again thrived although was inconspicuous among its other richer and more distinguished neighbours.

In 1726 John Wesley was elected a Fellow (a position which he held until his marriage in 1751 when he was obliged to resign). His presence brought the college to prominence, since members of the Holy Club met in his rooms and the college was regarded as the cradle of Methodism. His portrait still hangs in the Hall and his bust overlooks the front quadrangle. Following this fame came obscurity in the form of Edward Tatham, who became rector in 1792. He was a brusque Yorkshireman who became unpopular with his own Fellows as well as heads of other Oxford institutions (e.g. he opposed the conferral of an honorary degree on Edmund Burke) to the point where the college suffered a severe decline in numbers and prestige.

Even today, despite many additions over the years, the college still remains in many respects a classic example of a small 15th century college and is seen as a conservative institution which only admitted female students in 1979.

There is long-standing rivalry with neighbour Brasenose College, which was also founded by a Bishop of Lincoln, in that the two colleges share a tradition revived annually on Ascension Day. Legend has it that at one time a mob chased students through the town and the Lincoln porter only allowed his own students to pass, refusing entry to a Brasenose member who was subsequently killed by the mob. An alternative (although less colourful story) is that the student actually died as a result of a duel with a Lincoln student. As a penance on Ascension Day members of Brasenose College are invited through the one door connecting the two colleges, for free beer (said to be flavoured with ivy so as to discourage excessive consumption).

Famous alumni include Dr. Seuss, John le Carré and John Radcliffe (who later fell out with the college).

The *Inspector Morse* film crew never visited the college, but it has become a favourite with the *Lewis* production team. It doubles as Mayfield College in *Lewis: Life Born of Fire*, an un-named college part of the Radcliffe Observatory in *Lewis: Dark Matter*, the college (along with New College and Harrow School) where the quiz weekend was being held in *Lewis: Your Sudden Death Question* (the library being used on this occasion) and finally in *Lewis: Falling Darkness* where shots were taken from the library.

MAGDALEN COLLEGE & BRIDGE

One of the most frequent images of Oxford used by artists is that of Magdalen College as seen from Magdalen bridge. The latter spans the River Cherwell and may be the original 'ox ford'. A bridge has been here since 1004. During the Middle Ages bridge-hermits were employed to help travellers with any difficulties. It is thought that first bridge was of wood and was replaced only in the 16th century by a stone structure of around five hundred feet in length with arches every twenty-five feet. It is believed that William Waynflete, the founder of Magdalen College, may have paid for bridge repairs in the 15th century, and certainly by 1723 there are records to show that the University of Oxford was responsible for this task. However, this was not enough, as the bridge was later condemned as being dangerous and was consequently rebuilt between 1772 and 1778 to the design of John Gwynn. It was a toll bridge complete with a tollhouse and gates across the road. The balustrade was designed by John Townesend. Apart from widening in 1835 and again in 1882 the bridge remains much the same today.

Magdalen College owes its foundation to the aforementioned William Waynflete, who used the Hospital of St. John the Baptist, whose function it was to tend the sick and needy travellers, for a new college. By 1458 while he was Chancellor of England the number of brethren at the hospital had fallen to just five, which made it easy for Waynflete to suppress the hospital and transfer its site to a new college for the study of theology and philosophy. However, although building work did not start until 1474 the main buildings were completed by 1481, thanks to the generosity of Waynflete himself and several endowments (including that of Lord Cromwell) which made it the wealthiest college in Oxford. The college was successful and by 1565 had 132 'gentlemen commoners' along with their servants.

[Magdalen Bridge and college tower behind (date unknown)]

During the Civil War the college was most certainly royalist and even lent King Charles I the sum of £1,000. After the battle of Edgehill (which the Royalists lost), Oxford became a garrison town, with Magdalen tower being used as an observation point and stocked with missiles to defend the London road. When the Roundheads won the war the chapel was stripped and most of the remaining College Plate and ornaments were sold off or destroyed.

It was not until 1877 that sciences were allowed to be taught and 'ordinary commoners admitted'. Only after World War I was the emphasis placed on academic achievement over social or sporting attainment, and not until 1979 were women admitted.

Each May Day choristers sing an invocation to summer and 'according to an ancient custom, salute flora at four in the morning with vocal music of several parts' from the top of Magdalen tower. This custom probably originated in the 16th century, but by the 18th century listeners to the choir were in danger of being bombarded with rotten eggs and flour by undergraduates in the tower. Today the tradition continues, only at a slightly more civilised 6 a.m., and includes Morris Dancers, punting and champagne breakfasts.

The college is featured many times in the *Inspector Morse* series. Morse is attacked here by Ned and later attends a talk given by Tony Richards in *The Dead of Jericho*, while in *Greeks Bearing Gifts* this is where Morse dines and meets Randall Rees. It is also the setting of Arabella's ransacked room in *Twilight of the Gods*. In the final episode, *The Remorseful Day*, Lewis stands on a terrace overlooking the River Cherwell (with Colin Dexter making his usual cameo appearance this time in a wheelchair as part of a 'SAGA' type holiday group). The bridge is seen in passing in *The Wolvercote Tongue*, *The Settling of the Sun*, *Death is now My Neighbour*, once again in *The Remorseful Day*, and more recently in *Lewis: Reputation*. It would also appear to be the place to dispose of evidence since in *The Secret of Bay 5B* Henderson throws a tape from here into the river, while in *Dead on Time* it is Lewis who throws an incriminating tape (to protect Morse's feelings since it concerns his old love, Susan Fallon).

In *Lewis: Whom the Gods Would Destroy* Seymour College is a mixture of both Magdalen and Oriel colleges. The Principal's house, the quadrangle, cloisters and forecourt are all Magdalen College. Perhaps more memorable are the scenes in *Lewis: Allegory of Love* that take place by the river along Addison's Walk, which feature with a horse bolting in the opening shot and then later in the same episode as the location, where

Marina Hartner's body is found surrounded by a broken mirror. Interestingly these scenes were done during the filming of *Lewis: The Quality of Mercy* over a month later. Finally in the opening shots of *Lewis: Fearful Symmetry* Jessica Lake is seen cycling over the bridge.

MARTYRS' MEMORIAL

[The Martyrs' Memorial at St. Giles' (date unknown)]

The history of this memorial really begins in 1553 when Queen Mary came to the throne. She was a Roman Catholic and ordered Thomas Cranmer (Archbishop of Canterbury), Nicholas Ridley (Bishop of London) and Hugh Latimer (Bishop of Worcester) to appear before a commission in Oxford on a charge of Protestant heresies.

Thomas Cranmer had already been found guilty of treason for proclaiming Lady Jane Dudley to be Queen after entering the Tower of London with others on 10th July 1553, and also for sending men in arms to help the Duke of Northumberland against Queen Mary. He had been sentenced to be hanged, drawn and quartered for these crimes, but Mary also wanted him tried for the greater offence of heresy.

The trial started on 16th April 1554 in the Divinity School and took the form of a disputation conducted in Latin. Each of the accused were to defend their beliefs on the subjects of the 'Real Presence at the Mass', 'Transubstantiation' and the 'Mass as a sacrifice'. On 20th April all three were told that they had failed to prevail and that they should recant. They refused and thereby became heretics. Fortunately the burning of heretics had been repealed in 1547 and a new bill before Parliament to reverse this law was defeated by the House of Lords. It was then decided that they should be tried by the courts of the Papal Legate. Meanwhile a new Parliament re-enacted the heresy statutes. Cranmer was tried before the Pope's commissioners in September 1555 and the proceedings sent to Rome, during which time Cranmer was able to appeal. Ridley and Latimer were also tried, found guilty, excommunicated and burned at the stake on 16th October 1555 after refusing to recant. The burning took place in a ditch just outside the northern city wall. However, Cranmer, being an Archbishop, had to be 'degraded' by being ceremoniously stripped of his vestments first before he could be burned. He was made to watch the burning of Ridley and Latimer from a parapet in the city wall.

"Be of good comfort, Master Ridley; we shall this day light such a candle, by God's grace, in England as I trust shall never be put out," are the reported last heroic words of Latimer at the stake.

The eighty days given to Cranmer to appeal ran out in November 1555, but in January 1556 he did write a recantation. However, his accusers were not satisfied and demanded two more recantations to be written and sent to the Pope. In fact he was to write six recantations in all, but to no avail. On 21st March 1556 he appeared at the church of St. Mary the Virgin where he was to speak to the congregation and proclaim that he believed in the Catholic faith. He actually read out a speech repudiating his recantations. He was burnt shortly afterwards.

It was not until the 19th century that an appeal was launched to build a memorial for these martyrs. It was situated in St. Giles' on the site of the Robin Hood Inn and other houses on the north side of the church of St. Mary Magdalen. The monument was designed by Sir George Gilbert Scott and took two years to construct (1841 to 1843). The design was based on the 13th century Eleanor Cross at Waltham Cross, which was one of the crosses erected by King Edward I in memory of Queen Eleanor. The statues were carved by Henry Weekes and have Cranmer facing north holding his Bible marked May 1541. The significance of the

51

date is that this was when the Bible was allowed to be circulated by royal authority, something that Cranmer had long pleaded. Ridley faces east and Latimer faces west with his head bowed and arms crossed.

The inscription on the base reads: 'To the Glory of God, and in grateful commemoration of His servants, Thomas Cranmer, Nicholas Ridley, Hugh Latimer, Prelates of the Church of England, who near this spot yielded their bodies to be burned, bearing witness to the sacred truths which they had affirmed and maintained against the errors of the Church of Rome, and rejoicing that to them it was given not only to believe in Christ, but also to suffer for His sake; this in the year of our Lord, MDCCCXLI'.

The tourist party in *The Wolvercote Tongue* visit the Martyr's Memorial. It is there that Howard Brown makes his excuses to leave the guided tour and visit some interesting steam trains at the Didcot Railway Centre, while his wife keeps correcting poor old Cedric Downes, who is standing in as tour guide for Theodore Kemp. It also appears in *Deadly Slumber* and more recently in *Lewis: Reputation* where Lewis, having just returned to Oxford, says that nothing has changed since his departure, and yet is driven up to the memorial and then right into Beaumont Street only to be facing the Radcliffe Camera! There are further passing shots in *Lewis: Counter Culture Blues* and *Lewis: The Dead of Winter*, while it is featured twice in *Lewis: Fearful Symmetry* (with Robert Massey walking along St. Giles' and into the Ashmolean Museum via the side entrance, and later with the monument in the background as Lewis and Hobson talk).

MERTON COLLEGE

Walter de Merton was an only son with no fewer than seven sisters and thirteen first cousins, and it was the size of his own family that led him to establish an educational institution. He was a rich man himself and at his death in 1277 he had fifteen manors and pieces of land to his name. His first endowment was to be administered by Merton Priory and entirely devoted to the support of male members of his family, and by 1264 he had plans for an institution in Oxford to support twenty Fellows (hence Merton College does lay claim to being the oldest Oxford college, although at this time it had no buildings only a statute).

Merton himself had been Chancellor to both King Henry III and Edward I and during his service had drawn up the aforementioned statutes for an independent academic community that most importantly would be self-governing, with all endowments going straight to the Warden and Fellows (with the only right of intervention being by the Visitor or Archbishop of Canterbury). By 1274 when he retired from royal service there was an academic community consolidated at the present site of the college with a rapid programme of building taking place.

The initial acquisition included the parish church of St. John (which was superseded by the chapel when the former fell into 'a ruinous state') and three houses to the east of the church which now comprise the north range of Front Quadrangle. Walter also obtained permission from the king to extend from these properties south to the old city wall to form an approximately square site. The college continued to acquire other properties as they became available on both sides of Merton Street.

[The sundial in the Fellows' Garden (left) and the magnificent ironwork of St. Alban's Quadrangle (right)]

The strength of Merton College lay in the teaching of medicine and theology as well as the arts, with what became known as the Merton School making considerable contributions to the study of mechanics, geometry and physics throughout the Middle Ages.

Merton, unlike some other colleges picked its Fellows wisely since they had to be elected as vacancies became available and as resources allowed. Also all Fellows had to already hold a BA degree and were expected to complete a probationary period of a year before full admission to the college. Merton therefore became one of the most prestigious and wealthy of the Oxford colleges. For example in 1599 the college was able to speculate and purchase the manor of Gamlingay St. George in Cambridgeshire for £1,830 and from this and other rents was able to build a new large quadrangle. Indeed, perhaps because of the somewhat better academic standards expected here Merton men tended to gain positions of power and wealth and seldom forgot their old college in their return.

In 1548 the independent St. Alban Hall owned by the convent of Littlemore was purchased and incorporated into the college, although it continued as a separate institution until 1881 when it was finally annexed. During the Civil War the college was royalist to the extent that it provided both silver plate for the cause and accommodation for the Queen. However, the warden was suspected of supporting the parliamentarians, and for this reason the college is often cited as being the only one in Oxford to side with parliament, with the actual college being moved to London at this time and the Oxford buildings being commandeered by the Royalists.

The site of Merton College is rather hemmed in, with Merton Street and the old city wall providing barriers to the front and rear of the college and Corpus Christi College and the old Littlemore Priory on the remaining sides. Hence Merton was never able to develop its site further but instead has remained a place of exceptional learning, wealth and beauty. Since 2004 it has appeared top of the Norrington academic tables for Oxford seven times. Famous alumni include Sir Basil Blackwell, Sir Thomas Bodley, Randolph Churchill, T. S. Eliot, William Harvey and J. R. R. Tolkien.

From an *Inspector Morse* perspective two visits were made here. The first in *Service of All the Dead* when Morse talks with the Archdeacon as they walk through the Front and Mob Quadrangles, and the second in *The Infernal Serpent* at the very beginning when the Master and Dr. Dear leave in the rain for the Oxford Union and also at the very end when Hopkirk smashes up the flowerpots. The *Lewis* series has also visited in *Lewis: Old School Ties* and *Lewis: Your Sudden Death Question* when the college was used directly, and also outside in Merton Street for establishing shots in *Lewis: Life Born of Fire*, *Lewis: Dark Matter* and *Lewis: Wild Justice*. Most recently the college can be seen in *Endeavour: First Bus to Woodstock*, this being the college of Dr. Stromming.

MITRE HOTEL

Originally the Mitre Hotel was a public house in the High Street. It is one of only three ancient Oxford inns that have survived to the present day. It was built around 1300 and was owned by Philip de Wormenhale, who in 1310 became Mayor of Oxford. It is in fact the conglomeration of several buildings in both the High Street and Turl Street. On his death in 1314 the property passed to his widow, who subsequently married William of Bicester. In turn on his death the Mitre Hotel was assigned in part endowment of his chantry in All Saints Church, also situated in, the High Street. However, All Saints Church was itself used as an endowment for Lincoln College and hence to this day the Mitre Hotel remains the property of Lincoln College.

[The Mitre Hotel]

The landlords were all Catholics, and in the 17th century Mass was frequently celebrated on the premises. By 1671 there were coaches running from the Mitre Hotel to London three days a week. Indeed, *The City and University Guide* of 1824 says that 'Close to the front of the Market is The Mitre Inn, whence go well-regulated coaches to all parts of the Kingdom. Chaises are also kept at this Inn'.

Later it became a popular hotel, but since 1967 the Mitre Hotel has been a pubic house and restaurant only. The upper rooms are now used to accommodate members of Lincoln College.

In *Happy Families* Morse meets Lewis close to here and pays a visit to Alfred Rydale, whose solicitor's office is just a few doors away. Rydale is Lady Balcombe's solicitor and friend, and was present at her Birthday party after which Sir John Balcombe was found brutally murdered by a stonemason's tool.

The Last Enemy is an adaptation of the 1983 novel *The Riddle of the Third Mile.*

[The entrance to the Mitre]

Here Morse's toothache is one of the elements to survive the adaptation, as is the unknown torso found at Thrupp. At the conclusion of the novel Morse leaves the buffet to celebrate the new Master of Lonsdale College early, to spend time by himself at the Mitre Hotel. Another visitor to the Mitre is Margaret Bowman in *The Secret of Annexe 3* when she needs two whiskies to soothe her nerves before visiting the tower of St. Mary's Church on a mysterious mission. The exterior can also be seen in *Lewis: Counter Culture Blues.*

NEW COLLEGE

Until 1400 this college was known as St. Mary College of Winchester in Oxford, but changed its name to distinguish it from the other St. Mary's College that later became Oriel College. Originally it was one of the six theology colleges, and by far the largest, principally for those entering the clergy, with only those scholars from Winchester being eligible to become college Fellows. New College was the first to be based around a quadrangle that contained all the major buildings. The construction was overseen by the college founder, William of Wykeham, the Bishop of Winchester, who also was also responsible for the building of the royal lodgings at Windsor Castle. He was a shrewd businessman as well, for the site of the college was chosen because it could be bought cheaply as a number of small plots that had been particularly affected by plague, being described as 'full of filth, dirt, and stinking carcasses'. The foundation stone was laid on 5th March 1380, with the buildings being erected in increments between then and 1403, when the bell-tower was completed.

[The main entrance and Porters' Lodge from Holywell Quadrangle]

One of the most interesting buildings is the chapel, which is T-shaped, with an antechapel at right-angles to the nave. This allowed for worship in the nave while private Masses could be conducted in the antechapel, where disputations and elections were also held. The chapel was built in the Perpendicular style, though decoration was restrained. The original roof was probably a tiebeam construction, but today a taller hammerbeam roof designed by Sir George Gilbert Scott survives, along with sixty-two of the original misericords in the Fellows' stalls, many of which show rich images of Oxford life, from a doctor lecturing, to scholars fighting with daggers. The rest of the wooden features and the figures on the reredos belong firmly in the Victorian era.

The Protestant Reformation was felt in the College when in 1528 the then Warden, Dr. London, deprived John Quinbey of his Fellowship on account of his heresy. He was subsequently imprisoned in the bell-tower where he starved to death. While obeying the commands of King Henry VIII, which included the destruction of many of the college's precious manuscripts, the college remained a centre for the Catholic faith, which was to continue until Queen Elizabeth I purged many of the Catholic Fellows. In addition the chapel altar was removed, much of the Medieval glass destroyed, and the reredos plastered over. As a result the college was no longer seen as being at the forefront of religious leadership in Oxford.

However, the college continued to grow in size and even the Civil War did little to change the place, despite the cloisters acting as the main arsenal for the king's army, following the defeat at Edgehill in 1642. Cromwell did have fifty of the Fellows ejected, to be replaced by fifty-five new Fellows along with a new Warden, George Marshall, a Cambridge man. This was short-lived, for during the Restoration the college was again to thrive with the expulsion and appointment of yet more Fellows. Indeed, New College became the richest in revenues save for the colleges of Christ Church and Magdalen, although academically, with Fellowships being bought and sold, standards were to fall, with the college becoming more of a club where Fellows were 'much given to drinking and gaming and vain brutish pleasure' and where 'they degenerate in learning'.

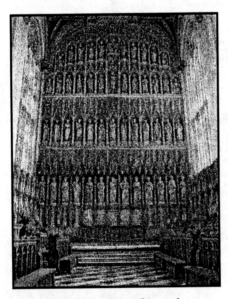

[The Chapel reredos and magnificent stone sculptures by J. L. Pearson]

There was at this time much building and redesigning taking place and nowhere more than in the chapel. Between 1736 and 1740 William Price of Hatton Garden restored the windows on the south side of the nave, while in 1765 William Peckitt of York repaired the north side and west window (the removed glass actually being sold to York Minster where it remains to this day). The Fellows disliked the new west window so much that in 1777 they had the glass moved to a window in the north-east of the nave, and commissioned Joshua Reynolds to design another west window, depicting the Nativity.

Further, between 1789 and 1794 James Wyatt made a plaster vault in the roof and replaced the reredos with plaster imitations of the originals (though these were in turn replaced during the Victorian era by ones in stone, whose niches were filled with sculptures by J. L. Pearson).

With refurbished buildings came more rigorous academic standards and a consequent rise in undergraduates from 1810, though for many years the college preserved its right of exempting its members from the University examinations. It was not until 1857 that various reforms (along with others over the next thirty years) were agreed upon, which brought the college into line with others. Today the college is particularly strong in the sciences, though it is interesting to note that female students were not admitted until 1979.

The original main (west) entrance to the college was via New College Lane (as opposed to Holywell Street) which runs from Catte Street under the bridge of Hertford College to Queen's Lane. Although *Inspector Morse* was never filmed within the college itself, Morse is seen in New College Lane in *The Wolvercote Tongue, Fat Chance, Happy Families, Absolute Conviction* and *Death is now My Neighbour*. Lewis visits the college chapel (in its guise as Seymour College) for the chamber music concert, and subsequently follows Sefton Linn from the chapel and is seen running after him up New College Lane in *Lewis: Whom the Gods Would Destroy*. New College Lane is also seen in *Lewis: Life Born of Fire* as the location where Lewis and Hathaway argue, *Lewis: And the Moonbeams Kiss the Sea, Lewis: The Quality of Mercy, Lewis: The Point of Vanishing* as where Lewis interviews the street sweeper, Alex Hadley, *Lewis: Wild Justice* in which the college in part doubles for the fictional St. Gerard's Hall, and finally this is also the location of Miranda Thornton's house in *Lewis: Generation of Vipers*.

ORIEL COLLEGE & SQUARE

Oriel College was founded by King Edward II, at the suggestion of his almoner, Adam de Brome, the charter being dated 12th April 1326 with a licence to found 'a certain college of scholars studying various disciplines in honour of the Virgin', along with the sum of £30 per annum. The king presented a large messuage known as *La Oriole* – hence the name of the college.

The hall was built in 1637 and has a most notable entrance portico surmounted by a parapet with the words *Regnante Carolo* (which was restored in 1897). Over the entrance are statues of the Virgin and Child, with those of King Edward II and King Charles I in canopied niches under a semi-circular pediment. Inside is one of the finest oak roofs in Oxford. The chapel that adjoins the hall was completed in 1642.

[The hall porch with its pierced parapet tracing the words *Renante Carolo* to commemorate King Charles I, in whose reign the quadrangle was completed]

The sympathies of the college Fellows during the Civil War was unclear. They were regarded with some suspicion by the Visitor appointed by Parliament in 1647, although the college did manage to maintain its independence at the cost of seven Fellows being expelled and replaced by what Dean Fell described as 'the dregs of the neighbour University'.

The 1700s were a time of change for the college. One undergraduate referred to 'frivolous lectures and unintelligible disputations', although it is fair to say that in general academic standards in Oxford remained low for most of the century. Oriel College did attract some transatlantic students at this time, who were in the main the sons of planters in Virginia, and one of them later came to regret giving a job to a young surveyor by the name of George Washington. Even so the college was able to expand during the century into a second quadrangle and also built the fine Senior Library to house a large gift of books. From 1780 to 1830 the college led the way in reforming academic standards in Oxford and in a religious revival, the so called Oxford Movement. The Oriel Fellowships were thrown open to competitive examination and many great names arrived, among them Dr. Thomas Arnold and the Blessed John Henry Newman. By the late 1800s, however, Oriel College was better known for prowess at rowing, soccer and cricket than in final exams and remained subdued during much of the 1900s, affected by two World Wars and the Great Depression, when the last estates were sold. However, since 1985 when women were allowed in the story is one of growth.

Famous alumni include Beau Brummel, Lord Fairfax, Sir Thomas More, Sir Walter Raleigh and Cecil Rhodes who in 1899 gave £100,000, free of all duty, to his old college for the extension of buildings to the High Street (the Rhodes Building) and an additional £10,000 to maintain 'the dignity of the High Table'.

Oriel College was featured in *The Silent World of Nicholas Quinn*, *The Ghost in the Machine*, *The Infernal Serpent* – in which Dr. Dear's funeral takes place in the chapel with lunch in the hall afterwards, *Deadly Slumber* and *Twilight of the Gods*. The Middle Common Room, one of the multicoloured houses in Oriel Square, became the music examination room (for the 'Endeavour Award') in *Lewis: Reputation*. Island Quadrangle was also used in the same episode. In fact this college is somewhat a favourite with the *Lewis* crew since it again appears in *Lewis: Whom the Gods Would Destroy* in the guise of Seymour College and also in *Lewis: Old School Ties* where the Porter's Lodge was utilised as that of Caroline's and Weller's college, and again in *Lewis: The Quality of Mercy* as the offices of the Oxford Alternative Press, the student newspaper (although the interior shots were done at Brunel University), while in *Lewis: The Point of Vanishing* Hope Ransome and Daniel Rattenbury both have rooms here (although the exterior shots for the former are actually of Balliol College). Finally in *Lewis: Dark Matter* various parts of the college were filmed, including scenes at the indoor shooting range

[Oriel Square (note the barriers which make this a quiet area for filming by day) with the row of multicoloured houses to the centre. Oriel College is just out of view to the right]

Outside the college is Oriel Square, formerly Canterbury Square, which is known for the various 18th century town houses, owned by the college, which are distinctive for their vivid individual colours that brighten the otherwise unremarkable features of the square. Perhaps the fact that Oriel Square is a no through road during the day, and therefore quiet, explains why so many scenes were filmed in this area.

Oriel Square may be seen in *The Dead of Jericho, Last Seen Wearing, The Ghost in the Machine, The Infernal Serpent, Absolute Conviction, Deadly Slumber, The Daughters of Cain.* In the *Lewis* series it has featured in *Lewis: Counter Culture Blues* and *Lewis: Wild Justice* so it should be no surprise if the surroundings look familiar to the reader. Its most recent appearance is in *Endeavour: First Bus to Woodstock* in which the young Morse goes and interviews Brian Lomax, the student from Australia, who is living in the corner property to the left of Oriel Square in the picture above.

OXFORD PRISON

In 1785 the county justices bought the old gaol in Oxford Castle and redeveloped it as a gaol and house of correction, under the supervision of George Moneypenny. There were two wings, one on each side of the keeper's house, for debtors and felons respectively. There was also a condemned cell in the Castle's St. George's tower. In 1788 the house of correction was added with separate wings for men and women. In 1819 and 1820 various alterations were carried out and an exercise yard added, but it was not until the 1850s that the prison was enlarged to hold a total of 400 inmates. The prisoners were occupied during the day by the use of the treadmill and the crank.

By 1945 the prison was seriously overcrowded but remained in operation, until a closure order came into force on 7th September 1996, as a local prison serving the Crown Courts of Oxford and Aylesbury, with an average population of 230 inmates. In 2006 it re-opened as a luxury hotel maintaining much of the original character.

[The interior of Oxford Prison. The one-time cells are now the hotel guest rooms and occasional scene of crime]

One evocative, and historically correct appearance in *Inspector Morse*, was in *The Wench is Dead*, as the site where the boatmen (wrongly) accused of the murder of Joanna Franks were hanged. The hotel also featured very prominently in *Lewis: Old School Ties* with a murder taking place in one of the bedrooms, while in *Lewis: Fearful Symmetry* various scenes were shot in the vicinity, with Oxford Castle clearly visible in the background, as are some of the bars on the old prison cells.

OXFORD RAILWAY STATION

[Two views of the latest characterless, but functional, Oxford railway station complete with a large bicycle parking area]

The story of the railway line to Oxford is one of vested interests. As early as 1837 the Great Western Railway proposed a line from Didcot to a station near Magdalen Bridge which would have gone parallel to Cowley Road. This was opposed by Christ Church College, who owned much of the land, and the City Corporation, who feared a loss in tolls from Folly Bridge if people started using the new railway. In addition the Oxford Canal Company also feared a loss in trade and so it was no great surprise that successive Bills before Parliament for the Oxford Railway were turned down in 1837, 1838 and 1840. Interestingly the University as a whole also objected to the railway on moral grounds. It will be recalled that one of the great opponents of all railways was the Duke of Wellington, who wanted to discourage the lower orders from 'moving about', and it should not be forgotten that he was Chancellor of the University at that time.

However, it soon became clear that the citizens of Oxford wanted a railway, since they were prepared to travel the one-and-a-half hours by stagecoach to Steventon, where a new station had been built. In 1843 the University dropped its opposition, on securing the right to enter any railway building and demand information about any passenger who 'shall be a Member of the said University or suspected of being such'. Further, the University was able to inform the railway about any Member of the University 'not having taken the Degree of Master of Arts or Bachelor in Civil Law' with the requirement that the railway would then 'refuse to convey such Member of the said University'. This applied even if the said 'Member may have paid his Fare'. There was also a list of approved places to which 'Junior Members of the University' were allowed to travel, and this did not include Ascot, which was seen as debauched due to its horseracing connections.

Only Wadham College now stood in the way of progress, but this was understandable since the Warden was also chairman of the Oxford Canal Company. The railway eventually reached Oxford in 1844 (and continued on to Banbury) but via a crossing at the Abingdon Turnpike Road rather than the planned bridge, due to the landowner erecting a house of timber frame and brown paper walls in order to win compensation. The terminus was Grandpont station. Tickets to London cost between six shillings (third class) and fifteen shillings (first class) which compared unfavourably with the five shillings stagecoach fare, although the journey was faster at just two hours and twenty minutes.

Following the Great Western's success, the London and North Western Railway also wanted access to the city, and in 1851 a new station opened in Rewley Road serving Bletchley, where passengers could change for trains to Euston, Birmingham and Cambridge (though it is not clear why anybody from Oxford would wish to go to the latter!).

Not to lose business in 1852 the Great Western Railway extended their line from Banbury to Birmingham and built a new station adjacent to Rewley Road. Grandpont station was closed to passengers, though it remained open as a goods yard until 1872.

The line was a success, and soon newer facilities such as toilets 'based on the latest scientific principles' were added. Much of the wooden structure remained until the 1970s when the station was rebuilt, leaving only some of the 1910 vintage roof girders. Some twenty years later the station was again rebuilt at a cost of £3 million and re-opened in 1990.

The old London and North Western Railway did not fare as well, as its line was taken over by the London, Midland and Scottish Railway in

65

1922 and in 1967 was closed to passengers altogether, though part of the station still remains as a Grade II listed building.

**[The up (London) platform has seen many an arrival
and departure of an *Inspector Morse* suspect]**

The station appears many times for the arrival and departure of suspects in the *Inspector Morse* episodes. In *The Wolvercote Tongue* it is Lewis who follows Howard Brown to the station and then on to the Didcot Railway Centre, where Morse joins them for an ice cream. A key clue is supplied by the railway in *The Ghost in the Machine* in which, following a (supposed) night at the opera in London Lady Hanbury returns, as does Morse, by train to Oxford, where she gives Betty Parker a lift. Lewis and Dobson find the tampered bicycle at the station in *Fat Chance*, while in *The Silent World of Nicholas Quinn* an alibi is (supposedly) established when Christopher Roope meets the Dean of Lonsdale College as they alight in Oxford.

There are passing shots of the station in *Second Time Around*, *Who Killed Harry Field?*, *The Daughters of Cain*, *The Wench is Dead*, and *The Remorseful Day*. In *Lewis: Whom the Gods Would Destroy* Ingrid Nielson and Dean Greely are both seen arriving here by train. However, the film crews often play tricks and in *Lewis: Allegory of Love* what is meant to be Oxford railway station is in fact that at Denham in Buckinghamshire.

OXFORD UNION

'Unique in that it has provided an unrivalled training ground for debates in the Parliamentary style which no debating society in any democratic country can equal' was how Harold Macmillan described the Oxford Union Society. It was founded in December 1825 out of the Oxford United Debating Society which had been founded in 1823.

[The Oxford Union]

Past officers of the Union have included five Prime Ministers (Gladstone, Salisbury, Asquith, Macmillan and Heath) as well as Cabinet Ministers, leading politicians, judges, bishops and distinguished people from all walks of life. The Union first met in rooms at Wyatt's, a picture dealers, but in 1852 bought a site in St. Michael's Street which has remained the permanent home for the society ever since. However, it was not until 1857 that the debating hall, now the old library, was built. Benjamin Woodward produced a Gothic room in brick with a gallery all round and two fireplaces back to back in the centre. The walls were painted by William Morris and Dante Gabriel Rossetti with scenes from *Morte d'Arthur*. Rossetti started with *Sir Lancelot's Vision of the Holy Grail* while Morris did *Tristram and Iseult* and also the ceiling on which he painted a vast pattern-work of grotesque creatures.

John Hungerford Pollen then joined the group and painted *King Arthur Receiving his Sword Excalibur*, followed by Edward Burne-Jones, who produced the *Death of Merlin*, and Arthur Hughes, who painted *Death of Arthur*, and finally Rodham Spencer Stanhope, who created *Sir Gawain and the Three Damsels at the Fountain*. The paintings were highly acclaimed but were unfortunately not to last, for they had been done on whitewashed walls that had not been properly prepared. Morris repainted the ceiling pictures in 1875, further restoration being performed in 1930 by Professor Tristram.

However, despite these attempts most of the murals are too faded to be recognisable. William Riviére was commissioned to paint *Arthur's First Victory, Arthur's Education under Merlin* and *Wedding of Arthur and Guinevere* in three of the empty bays.

In 1863 a library was added to the old debating hall and in 1878 a new debating hall was constructed. The new hall is in similar style to the old hall with a gallery for visitors. A new Gothic library, dining room and steward's house were also built between 1910 and 1911. Today the Oxford Union has the largest lending library within the University.

The debates that have taken place over the years are noted for their wit and have included all manner of famous people. The best known, and certainly most controversial, debate was in February 1933 when the motion 'that this House will in no circumstances fight for its King and its Country' was passed by two hundred and seventy-five votes to one hundred and fifty-three. Randolph Churchill later moved, unsuccessfully, that the debate should be expunged from the minute book. On 2nd May 1968 the Queen attended her first debate. The first woman to address the Oxford Union was Mrs. Millicent Garrett Fawcett, but it was not until 1968 that a woman, Geraldine Jones, became President. The most notable female President was Benazir Bhutto. Finally it was in 1986 that, for the first time, the President, Librarian and Treasurer were all women.

In *Greeks Bearing Gifts* Morse finds himself as a one-man audience in the Oxford Union debating chamber listening to a talk by Randall Rees. At the beginning of *The Infernal Serpent* Morse is hurrying through the rain to listen to Dr. Dear but never actually gets to hear his sensational revelations as Dear is murdered on his way.

In *Lewis: Old School Ties* Nicky is seen giving a lecture to students here, while good use of this location was also made in *Lewis: The Point of Vanishing*, and it is also where visiting American academic Paul Yelland is heckled at the entrance in *Lewis: The Indelible Stain*.

68

OXFORD UNIVERSITY REAL TENNIS CLUB

[The only real tennis court still in use in Oxford]

Real tennis, one of the oldest racket sport games in the world, its name derived from the French *réal* meaning 'royal', has been played in Oxford since 1450. It is played in a four-walled court, divided by a net as in lawn tennis, but the walls are in play. Features of the court are the penthouses, dedans, tambour, grille and chase lines. Several such courts existed in Oxford at Queen's, Lincoln and Christ Church Colleges along with a further two at Smith's Gate (now part of Hertford College), as well as in Alfred Street, Oriel Street and Merton Street.

In 1508 four citizens were fined sixpence each for keeping unlicensed courts, while in 1643, during the Civil War, King Charles I sought and obtained permission from Parliament for material for a tennis suit to be sent from London so that he might play the game in Oxford.

However, despite the royal patronage the game's popularity declined and one by one the various courts closed, so that today only the ones at Oriel and Merton Colleges still exist, though the former has not been used for tennis since the 1850s, having most recently been converted into undergraduate accommodation. The Merton College court, which hosts the Oxford University Real Tennis Club, was rebuilt in 1798 and is the second oldest court still in play in England (the oldest being that at Hampton Court, once used by King Henry VIII). The club still thrives, with two professionals in attendance, and lays claim to the fact that former world champion, Chris Ronaldson, learned the game on this very court. As with the more famous University Boat Race, there has been an annual real tennis competition between Oxford and Cambridge since 1858.

In *Lewis: Old School Ties* the real tennis court makes a memorable appearance, as it is where Lewis and Hathaway arrest David Harvey and Chloe during their game towards the end of the episode. Lewis hasn't actually grasped the distinction between real and lawn tennis and comments to Hathaway that it must be digital tennis that they play at Wimbledon if this is real tennis.

PARK TOWN

[Park Town where Lewis notes that Oxford roofs do sometimes curve]

Park Town is one of the most well-known streets in central North Oxford, and was also one of the earliest planned suburban developments in the area.

The Park Town Estate Company was formed in September 1857, through the efforts of Samuel Lipscomb Seckham. The elegant houses and gardens that resulted were originally surrounded by ornamental iron railings. Unfortunately, many of these were removed for the war effort to manufacture guns and ships in World War I. Park Town includes two crescents of town houses, surrounding communal gardens, together with a number of larger villas.

Miss Sarah Angelina Acland, daughter of Sir Henry Wentworth Acland, lived at No. 10 for a time. Her interest in colour photography at the turn of the century produced a number of interesting early examples, which are held at the Museum of the History of Science in central Oxford. This is in stark contrast to the 'glamour' photographic interests of Alisdair McBryde, who is interviewed here by Morse and Lewis in *The Way Through the Woods*.

Indeed, the location of the house is not certain, for the only clue to the person who has a surname starting with the letter 'M' comes from Lewis, who notes that one of Karen Anderson's photographs shows a house with a curved roof, which from his local knowledge he knows must be Park Town (although in the book it is Morse who makes this connection). Later Morse and Lewis are seen arriving here in the Jaguar and parking close to Seckham Crescent in The Terrace before asking a conveniently present postman for the address of anybody with the correct surname initial.

PITT RIVERS & UNIVERSITY MUSEUMS

The University Museum of Natural History came about as a consequence of a meeting held in 1849, which resolved that a building should be erected to bring together all 'the materials explanatory of the organic beings placed upon the globe'. It was not until 20th June 1855 that the foundation stone was laid, and five years later that the building was complete. Almost immediately it was a place of controversy since the British Oxford Association decided to meet there, and it is recorded that on that occasion the fundamentalist Bishop of Oxford, Samuel Wilberforce, argued with Professor Thomas Huxley about Darwin's theory of evolution.

The architect of the building was Benjamin Woodward of the Dublin firm of Sir Thomas Deane, Son and Woodward, who produced a fine Gothic structure much influenced by John Ruskin, whose *Stones of Venice* is clearly evident in the design of the Museum. It is approached through an elaborately decorated portal, carved in marble, and opens into a large square court, divided into three main aisles by iron pillars supporting a glass roof. The stone columns of the arcades are themselves exhibits, each being hewn from a different British rock.

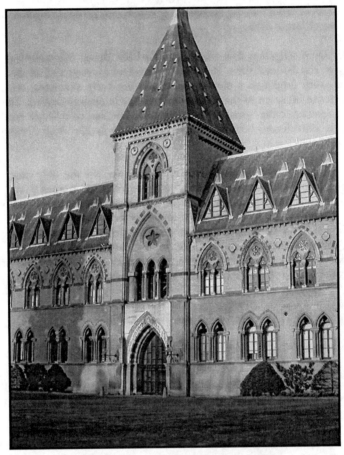

[The University Museum of Natural History within which is the Pitt Rivers Museum]

The wrought-ironwork embellishing the spandrels between the arches of the main aisles 'is formed into branches', in the words of the Museum guide, 'with leaves, flowers and fruits of lime, chestnut, sycamore, walnut, palm and other trees and shrubs, and the leaves of many different plants are incorporated in the capitals. The carved stone capitals of the columns and piers of the arcades represent a series of plants, often with birds and animals too, and are remarkable in that the stonemasons, including the colourful, mercurial O'Shea brothers, conceived as well as executed the designs themselves, on the basis of actual specimens provided by the Botanic Garden'. The O'Sheas, though, fell out with the dons, exasperated by their interference, but not before they had carved likenesses of members of the Convocation between parrots and owls. Although these were ordered to be obliterated they are still visible in part.

Francis Skidmore was paid to start the wall-frescoes and complete the carvings. However, money ran out and so the building was never finished as planned. Soon after opening, the departments of astronomy, geometry, experimental physics, mineralogy, chemistry, geology, zoology, anatomy, physiology and medicine all moved here. The building soon became inadequate in size and was used principally to house the scientific collections. There are four curators who are also involved in teaching and research activities. Today the museum holds the collections of the explorer, William Burchell, and of William Buckland, the geologist, a collection of osteological and physiological material from Christ Church College and a huge collection of insects (over three million specimens) and crustaceans presented to the museum by the Reverend F. W. Hope.

The Pitt Rivers Museum, established in 1884, is housed in a building adjoining the University Museum of Natural History, through which it is entered. The founding collection of some twenty thousand ethnographic and archaeological objects was given to the University by General Augustus Henry Lane Fox Pitt Rivers, who stipulated that a museum be built to house it. Henry Balfour, the museum's first curator, developed and greatly expanded the scope of the collections, which include photographs, manuscripts and sound recordings.

In a sense, anthropology as an academic subject in Britain may be said to have originated here, for the first lecturer ever to hold a post in that subject in a British university, Sir Edward Burnett Tylor, was appointed to lecture in the Pitt Rivers Museum, starting in the 1880s. Museum staff have continued to teach cultural anthropology since that time.

Today the Pitt Rivers Museum is considered to house one of Europe's finest ethnographic collections. These collections are from all parts of the world and are arranged to illustrate the history, typology, distribution and technology of the world's principal arts and industries, excluding in theory the products of mass production. Among the subjects particularly well presented are masks and other sculptural forms, musical instruments, textiles, arms and armour, religious and ritual objects, jewellery, amulets and charms, boats and boat models, costumes, pottery and lamps. Collections of historical significance include the artefacts brought back from Captain Cook's second voyage to the Pacific, the original Pitt Rivers Collection of ethnography and archaeology, a fine Benin collection from West Africa, and early North American and Arctic collections brought back by 18th and 19th century explorers. On a regional basis the traditional material culture of Africa and the Pacific are notable among the Museum's holding.

The objects in the Pitt Rivers Museum are displayed typologically, grouped by function or purpose rather than by geographical or cultural origin. This unusual layout was developed from Rivers' theory about the evolution of ideas. Today this approach reveals the diverse cultural solutions that have been found to common human problems. Many of the objects are beautiful and rare, but most are simple, everyday objects that reveal how humans have lived and thought. Such material was often not treasured or preserved elsewhere and is part of the Pitt Rivers' unique quality. Although the museum has changed a good deal over the last hundred years, the cluttered cases and original small handwritten labels help it retain its famous Victorian atmosphere.

**[The murder weapon from *The Daughters Of Cain*
(illustration reproduced by kind permission of the Pitt Rivers
Museum)]**

In *The Daughters of Cain* Ted Brooks originally worked as a scout at Wolsey College, but he was forced to leave due to his 'hushed-up' drug dealing, which resulted in a student suicide. He then found employment at the Pitt Rivers Museum, where he stole the knife bearing the legend 'Knife, Bartose, Northern Rhodesia. Given in 1919 to Bishop May by Zeta III, Paramount Chief and son of Cewanika'.

Brooks took the knife to kill Dr. McClure and hoped to return it before it was missed. Brooks could not effect the return, however, as he was too 'busy' recovering from a heart attack in hospital. The daughters of Cain then conceived their plan to kill Ted Brooks with the same weapon. The roguish schoolboy, Kevin Costyn, was persuaded to break into the knife cabinet at a pre-arranged time, to give an apparently much later date and time for the theft and therefore give the daughters of Cain an alibi.

The University Museum of Natural History provided the backdrop for the climax in *Lewis: Expiation*. It was used for the internal shots where Hugh shows Izzy and Anna the shrunken heads (actually in the Pitt Rivers Museum), and also for the chase scenes ending in the main tower. However, the scenes in the tower itself were just a studio set. Further filming has taken place here in *Lewis: The Gift of Promise*.

RADCLIFFE CAMERA & SQUARE

[The Radcliffe Camera]

After John Radcliffe's death in 1714 it took over twenty years of negotiations to clear the site for the building of the library for which he had left £40,000 in his will. The rotunda form was proposed by Hawksmoor, but it was the design of James Gibbs which was eventually preferred. The building, began in 1737, was completed in 1748 and opened in 1749 by Dr. William King, the Vice-Chancellor and Principal of St. Mary Hall. The building is believed to be the first round library in the country, and was originally intended to be a science library, though today the books found there are mainly devoted to the arts. The plasterwork in the splendid domed upper room is by Joseph Artari, Charles Stanley and Thomas Roberts. The square is the 'heart of Oxford' and according to Sir Nikolaus Pevsner 'is unique in the world'. He later added, 'or, if that seems a hazardous statement, it is certainly unparalleled at Cambridge'. It was at one time condemned due to the large size of its pebbles, which were ruinous to shoes. The defeat of Napoleon was celebrated here in 1814 by a dinner given to four thousand poor people.

Ted Brooks' blood-stained bike was found against the railings in Radcliffe Square in *The Daughters of Cain*. Ted Brooks has a murderous disagreement with Dr. Felix McCure, after which he suffers a heart attack and is forced to abandon his bike and take a taxi home. Being such a notable Oxford location it is not surprising to find passing shots of Radcliffe Square and Camera in *The Dead of Jericho*, *The Settling of the Sun*, *The Last Bus to Woodstock*, *The Ghost in the Machine*, *Absolute Conviction*, *Twilight of the Gods*, *The Way Through the Woods* and *Death is now My Neighbour*.

Naturally Radcliffe Square is also seen in the *Lewis* series, most notably in *Lewis: Expiation* as Lewis and Stephanie return to her car after going to Gee's (a well known Oxford restaurant). Interestingly Gee's was not used in filming, another restaurant in Summertown being used instead and the name being changed to Dee's. The pavement café frequented by Lewis and Laura Hobson in *Lewis: And the Moonbeams Kiss the Sea* was actually the café garden in the University Church of St. Mary the Virgin at the far end of Radcliffe Square. *Lewis: Music to Die For* used part of the square as a backdrop for some general shots of Oxford, as did *Lewis: The Point of Vanishing* in which Lewis and Laura Hobson walk and talk, while in the closing shots of *Lewis: Life Born of Fire* the viewer may spot Colin Dexter dressed as a don (but in a Cambridge gown) traversing the square while Lewis and Hathaway talk. It again features in *Lewis: The Mind Has Mountains*, while in *Lewis: Generation of Vipers* Miranda Thornton meets her former student here.

76

RADCLIFFE OBSERVATORY

[The Radcliffe Observatory at Green Templeton College]

Located in the Woodstock Road, the Radcliffe Observatory was built for Oxford University with a grant from the trustees of the estate of John Radcliffe. The design was started by Henry Keene in 1772 but completed after his death by James Wyatt in 1794. It has been said that architecturally at least this is the finest building of its kind in Europe. The building is surmounted by a version of the Tower of the Winds, the octagonal horologium in Athens (built around 100 BC by Andronicus of Cyrrhus for measuring time). At the top are Hercules and Atlas supporting a globe, while below there are reliefs above the first floor windows, comprising the signs of the zodiac. The observatory is made up of just three main rooms, one per floor, and ceased to be used for its intended purpose in 1935 due to the urban development of the city.

Since then it was used as office and laboratory space for various medical departments until the Nuffield Institute for Medical Research moved to the John Radcliffe Hospital in 1976, when the building became empty. However, currently it belongs to Green Templeton College, where it has become a Common Room. Any visitor expecting to see scientific instruments inside will be sadly disappointed since none are present, although some are to be found in the Museum of the History of Science in Broad Street.

The building, though, reverted to its original function for the filming of *Lewis: Dark Matter* in which Professor Andrew Crompton, an amateur astronomer, is found dead in the observatory after visiting a priest for confession. Again the viewer should not be fooled, as all the internal shots showing equipment were actually done at the University of London Observatory at Mill Hill.

RANDOLPH HOTEL

[The elegant 1899 iron porch]

The hotel, which has 109 bedrooms, takes its name from the Randolph Gallery which stood opposite and which, in turn, took its name from the Reverend Dr. Francis Randolph, who was one of the principal benefactors of the Ashmolean Museum. The architect was William Wilkinson. The hotel opened on 17th February 1866 when a local newspaper reported:

> Entering by the portico in Beaumont Street, the visitor notices the mosaic flooring of the hall, the conservatory in the rear, and a massive staircase of Portland stone, leading to the various landings and corridors. The railing is of iron, with ornamental pillars and timber coping, the stairs being of a width recalling the baronial mansions of older time, and doubly carpeted.

In 1899 the iron porch and ballroom were added by H. W. Moore, and a further extension made in 1952. The hotel has always been a 'first-class Hotel for families and gentlemen' containing 'many handsome suites of rooms with very charming prospects' being fitted with 'an American elevator' and supplied 'throughout with Electric Lighting' as stated in a publicity brochure from 1910. In 2007 it received its fifth star.

In addition an omnibus met all the most important trains and there were stabling facilities adjoining the hotel as well as a large garage. According to the same brochure a suite of rooms cost between twenty-one and forty-two shillings a night, with a single room costing between three and six shillings a night.

[The Randolph Hotel from a 1930s advertisement]

The Jewel that was Ours (based on *The Wolvercote Tongue*) finds a group of American tourists at the Randolph Hotel as part of their 'historic cities of England tour'. In room 310, the Wolvercote Tongue vanishes, and its owner, Laura Stratton (Poindexter in the television dramatisation) is found dead, apparently from a coronary. Various other scenes were filmed here, including the Medieval dinner that occurred during the same 'time-frame' as the murder of Dr. Theodore Kemp. In the novel, Morse has an ill-fated date with Sheila Williams at twelve noon in the foyer, but she is already in the Chapters Bar, being 'very interested' in a younger man when Morse arrives!

The hotel was also featured in *The Infernal Serpent* and *Second Time Around*. In *The Wench is Dead* Adele Cecil has tea with Strange here and pleads for him to give an assistant to the bedridden Morse to investigate the historical murder of Joanna Franks. In *The Remorseful Day* the scheming Harrison family have dinner in the restaurant, while also in that episode Morse is served a drink in the bar (now The Morse Bar) by Ailesh Hurley, who was the long-time bar manager at the Randolph Hotel and a local celebrity much missed since her untimely death in 2005. In 2012 a portrait of Colin Dexter was unveiled in the bar.

In *Lewis: Whom the Gods Would Destroy* Lewis and Hathaway enter the hotel and question Ingrid (who is a hotel guest) in the restaurant. The hotel has a more prominent role in *Lewis: Allegory of Love* as both where Marina Hartner works, and where Dorian Crane's book launch takes place (and not least of all where Colin Dexter can be seen exiting during his Hitchcock-like appearance in this episode). However, the interior shots were done at Templeton, a conference centre at Roehampton near London, the clue being the fine gardens visible just outside the function room where the book launch is taking place. The Randolph Hotel has no such gardens.

The interior, including the Morse Bar, was used in *Lewis: The Quality of Mercy* as where Simon Monkford's luggage was apparently stolen. It later transpires that he is not only a small time conman, but also the person responsible for the death of Lewis's wife in a driving hit and run accident. Most recently Vernon Oxe, the music promoter (who is rather curiously played by Simon Callow, who also appeared as the unfortunate Dr. Theodore Kemp in *The Wolvercote Tongue*) stays here in *Lewis: Counter Culture Blues*. However, the interior shots of his room are actually at The Bentley Hotel in London, though good use is made of both the exterior and interior of the Randolph Hotel as well.

ROTHERMERE AMERICAN INSTITUTE

[A decidedly modern look for an Oxford Institution]

The Rothermere American Institute, squashed between Mansfield College and Rhodes House in South Parks Road, is an international centre of excellence dedicated to the interdisciplinary and comparative study of the United States, which provides a home in Oxford for students and scholars of American history, politics and culture. Former President of the United States, William Jefferson Clinton, officially opened the institute in front of four hundred guests on Friday 25th May 2001. It is named after Lord Rothermere, the third Viscount Rothermere, who had originally had the vision to create an institution of this kind to act as a cultural bridge between Europe and America.

Every year, the institute hosts more than a hundred seminars, workshops, conferences and lectures, which attract leading scholars, students, policy-makers and public figures from around the world to debate and study the United States. The Vere Harmsworth Library, housed within the institute, has the finest academic collections in American history, politics and government outside the United States.

81

Two notable features of the institute are the glass sculpture by the artist Julian Stocks, depicting the relationship between Great Britain and America, and, outside, the Princess Margaret Memorial Garden, opened by Her Majesty the Queen in 2006.

As far as filming goes it is the award-winning architecture of the building, designed by Kohn Pedersen Fox architects, that is the deciding factor, for it has been used several times in the *Lewis* series when something in a modern style is required. It first became the science block in *Lewis: Falling Darkness* and more recently Ganza's office in *Lewis: The Mind Has Mountains*.

SACKLER LIBRARY

[The Doric entrances to the Sackler Library (left)
and Wendy Spencer's residence (right)]

The Sackler Library was completed in 2001 and opened on 24th September of that year, replacing the former library of the Ashmolean Museum. The Library is located at No. 1 St. John Street, to the rear of the Ashmolean Museum and was founded with a generous donation by the multi-millionaire Dr. Mortimer Sackler.

The building was designed by architects Robert Adam and Paul Hanvey, and is distinctive in that the central block is circular. It is appropriate to its classical purpose, as one of the outer walls is decorated with a mock-

82

classical frieze. In addition, the entrance is based upon the Doric Temple of Apollo at Bassae, first excavated by Charles Robert Cockerell, the man who designed the Ashmolean Museum, though the façade does not really fit in with the rest of the terrace houses in the street.

The Sackler Library is one of the principal research libraries of the University of Oxford and specialises in archaeology, art history, and classics (ancient history and literature). It incorporates the collections of the former Ashmolean Library (including the Griffith Institute Library and the Western Art Library), the Classics Lending Library, the Eastern Art Library, and the History of Art Library.

Of course it could not be used in the filming of *Inspector Morse* since it did not exist at the time, but the producers of *Lewis* found a good, if rather strange, use for it in *Lewis: Music to Die For* where the entrance became that to the Portobello Club, where silence is certainly not the order of the day. Filming can be deceiving, though, for the supposed rear of the Portobello Club was actually shot at Trinity College, while the interior scenes were captured at the Cobden Club in London over a three day period. The building reprised its role in *Lewis: The Gift of Promise*.

St. John Street does have one connection with Inspector Morse for it was at No. 22 that Wendy Spencer lived. Those who are familiar with the Colin Dexter books, and in particular *The Riddle of the Third Mile*, will know that this is the postgraduate student with whom Morse fell in love with half-way through his third year at St. John's College reading classics. Indeed, it was this love affair with the girl from St. Hilda's College that led to Morse going down from Oxford having failed his degree, and thus becoming one of the 'Greats'. Maybe readers should be thankful to Wendy Spencer, for it was only once Morse had broken off the relationship after a year and become 'a withdrawn and silent young man, bitterly belittled, yet not completely broken of spirit' that he took the advice of his dying father, 'who suggested that his only son might find a niche in the police force'.

In *Endeavour: First Bus to Woodstock*, Morse, driving his boss's Jaguar, has stopped at the traffic lights. Fred Thursday asks him where he would like to be in twenty years time, and Morse looks into the driver's mirror and sees the face of John Thaw, just before the end credits roll, to the *Inspector Morse* theme tune. It is entirely appropriate that this scene was filmed at the corner of St. John Street and Pusey Street, with No. 22 clearly in shot as he drives off.

ST. ALDATE'S POLICE STATION

[St. Aldate's police station]

St. Aldate's is probably Oxford's oldest street, since it leads from the River Thames to the highest part of the city at Carfax. Towards the river end will be found the police station, conveniently opposite the new Crown Courts.

It has been estimated that there are about one hundred and fifty thousand bicycles in use in Oxford – and three thousand of them are stolen each year. The police have a special Cycles Department at St. Aldate's police station, where recovered bicycles are kept in a large store. Professional cycle theft is common and cyclists are now encouraged to have their postcode stamped on their bicycles. Many such bicycles recovered in London and elsewhere have been identified as having been stolen in Oxford. The police station store contains an average of four hundred stolen or abandoned bicycles. In 1986 alone the police recovered one thousand four hundred and eighty-nine machines. Every day nearly fifty people visit the store, which manages to return eight out of ten bikes to their owners. Those which cannot be identified are eventually sold off in job lots, raising around £5,500 each year.

Although most of Morse's investigations are Oxford-based, as a detective he would have had offices at Kidlington CID, and hence not have known St. Aldate's that well. However, he did take up residence here in *Service of All the Dead* when Chief Inspector Bell is removed from the case by Strange.

Surprisingly, the only filming that took place here was in *The Dead of Jericho* and *The Way Through the Woods* when Morse is criticised by Strange and, like Chief Inspector Bell, taken off the case.

Most of the actual 'police station' shots in the series were at a now redeveloped Territorial Army centre in Harefield, on which a housing estate now stands, bearing the road names Morse, Lewis, Dexter and Childs (the Executive Producer). In 2006 a plaque, sponsored by The Inspector Morse Society, was unveiled by Colin Dexter at St. Aldate's commemorating the link between Inspector Morse and the Thames Valley Police.

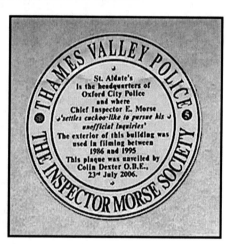

[The plaque at St. Aldate's]

SAINT MARY THE VIRGIN CHURCH

The University Church of St. Mary the Virgin can justifiably be said to be at the heart of the city and university. For a start it is located at the very centre of the old walled city, and in Medieval times, when the city had no university buildings of its own, the scholars lived among their teachers in houses and adopted St. Mary's church as its centre. Indeed, as well as being a parish church, by the early 13th century the building was also the seat of university government and academic disputation, and the place where the degrees were awarded. A century later, as the various colleges were being founded, more room was needed, and so the Old Congregation House at the north-east side of the church, abutting the tower, was built with the help of money endowed by Bishop Cobham specifically to house his books. Hence the upper room now became the university library, with the books chained in place, along with the university chest (literally since this is where the university's money was kept in a chest), while the lower room (now the café) was the university's parliament. This practice remained in place until the middle of the 17th century, although today this is still the church where the university worships, with the formal university sermon being preached here in front of the Vice-Chancellor and Proctors on two Sundays each term.

[The building that is the very heart of Oxford, circa 1814]

The church also has a connection with the three Oxford martyrs (Latimer, Ridley and Cranmer) who were first tried in the chancel in April 1554, with Ridley and Latimer being tried here a second time in 1555 before being burnt at the stake on the 16th October the same year for their rejection of the doctrine of transubstantiation. Another famous figure associated with the church is John Wesley, the founder of Methodism, who during his days as a Fellow of Lincoln College gave some of his most notable and stirring sermons here, including one in 1744 in which he denounced the 'laxity and sloth' of the senior members of the university. Not an entire surprise to him, then, that following this sermon he was never asked to preach here again! He was in no way regretful of his actions, writing 'I have preached, I suppose, the last time in St. Mary's. Be it so. I am now clear of the blood of these men. I have fully delivered my soul'.

In 1828 St. Mary's welcomed a new vicar, John Newman, who was a Fellow at Oriel College and thought by many to be the most intelligent man in Oxford, with the consequence that undergraduates flocked to his sermons. Matthew Arnold, an undergraduate at that time, wrote, 'Who could resist the charm of that spiritual apparition, gliding in the dim afternoon light through the aisles of St. Mary's, rising into the pulpit, and then, in the most entrancing of voices breaking the silence with words and thoughts which were a religious movement, subtle, sweet, mournful?' It was however, the Assize Sermon on the 14th July 1833, preached by John Keble, which is considered to have launched the famous Oxford Movement in which Newman's leadership was so central. However, by 1843, Newman had become disillusioned with Anglicanism and resigned from St. Mary's. He was soon to be accepted into the Roman Catholic faith, and in 1879 became one of its cardinals.

Today visitors can walk around the Adam de Brome Chapel (which is furnished as a courtroom reflecting its earlier use) and the Chancel where the aforementioned Oxford martyrs were tried, take refreshment in the coffee shop location in the vaults, or, for the more energetic, climb the tower for panoramic views of the city. Indeed, it was for some of those establishing sweeping shots of the Oxford skyline that the Inspector Morse production crew used this facility, not least in *The Silent World of Nicholas Quinn* and *The Settling of the Sun*.

The *Lewis* team have also visited, but mainly as a place for Lewis to take coffee, as in *Lewis: And the Moonbeams Kiss the Sea*, *Lewis: The Gift of Promise* and *Lewis Generation of Vipers*.

87

SAINT MICHAEL AT THE NORTH GATE

[The oldest building in Oxford is the Saxon tower of St. Michael's]

The Saxon tower was probably built around 1050, making this Oxford's oldest building. As the name suggests, the location is at the ancient North Gate of the city, although the tower was not a defensive one but more a look-out post. Later in its history the tower was connected on its west side to a building above the North Gate known as the Bocardo Prison, and it was here that the three Oxford Martyrs were imprisoned prior to their burning at the stake. Indeed, Cranmer's cell door is now an exhibit in the church tower.

The church has always been closely associated with Lincoln College since its foundation in 1427, at which time St. Michael's was appropriated to the college with successive chaplains up to the 19th century all being appointed by the college.

One of the stained glass windows dating from 1290 depicts St. Michael the Archangel carrying a shield with a unique cross, which the church has since adopted as its symbol. Other windows depict the Virgin Mary, St. Nicholas and St. Edmund of Abingdon. The church also contains a fine 17th century chest in which were kept various parish documents. Interestingly, it has three locks and could only be opened if all three key holders were present. The documents date back to 1404 and give great insight to the times. For instance, during the Civil War soldiers were billeted here, and the accounts show a cost of ten shillings and six pence 'for cleansing the Church and perfewminge it after the soldiers was lodged in it a week'.

When All Saints church, the former City Church (meaning that this is where the Mayor and Corporation of Oxford formally worship, whereas the University formally worships at the University Church of St. Mary the Virgin fronting Radcliffe Square) was converted into a library for Lincoln College, it fell to St. Michael's to carry on this role.

In 1953 the church was nearly destroyed by fire, thought to be the work of an arsonist. Actually this may have been a blessing in disguise, since the church was then closed for a year and not only restored but remodelled to become a brighter more friendly place. In 1986 the tower was opened up so that the ground floor now houses a library and the 'crying room' where children can play without disturbing services, while on the first floor is the treasury and above that the clock room, the upper and lower bell galleries (with some of the bells dating from 1668) and finally the roof which affords the public some spectacular views of Oxford.

The one piece of filming to take place here to date was done in September 2009 when it appears as the exterior of the theatre in *Lewis: Falling Darkness*.

SHELDONIAN THEATRE & EMPERORS' HEADS

It was Gilbert Sheldon, Chancellor of the University, who commissioned and in doing so gave his name to this theatre. It was meant to be a building in which university business could be enacted, including ceremonies which had previously taken place in the University Church of St. Mary the Virgin. Sheldon gave about fourteen and a half thousand pounds for the construction, which was designed by a young architect friend of his by the name Christopher Wren, at that time the Savilian Professor of Astronomy. It is, in part, inspired by the open-air Theatre of Marcellus in Rome and being classical in nature was said at the time to be revolutionary, since it was like no other Oxford building. Completed in 1669, it was constructed from high quality stone in the lower half, but cheaper Headington stone elsewhere as money ran out. This did not last as well and needed extensive renovation between 1959 and 1960.

The roof is of special interest since it allowed a span of seventy feet by eighty feet without supporting crossbeams. This was suggested to Wren by the mathematician John Wallis, who had been appointed Professor of Geometry in 1649. Originally the roof had dormer windows, but in 1838 these were replaced by the octagonal cupola designed by Edward Blore. The theatre holds two thousand seated people in tiers, and has an allegorical ceiling painting by Robert Streeter, sergeant painter to King Charles I, representing *Truth*, surrounded by *Justice, Law, Music, Geometry, Drama, Architecture* and *Astronomy*, triumphing over *Envy, Hatred* and *Malice*. The woodwork includes a fine Chancellor's throne and two orators' pulpits, and there is also an organ dating from 1877.

There is also a large room over the ceiling that was the original headquarters of the Oxford University Press before it moved to the adjacent Clarendon Building. Books printed during this time have the inscription *E Teatro Sheldoniano*. Today the theatre is used for *Encaenia* (a meeting of Convocation presided over by the Chancellor on the Wednesday in the ninth week of the Trinity Term), degree ceremonies, voting by Convocation and occasional concerts.

[Two Emperors and the Sheldonian Theatre]

Christopher Wren commissioned William Byrd, an Oxford stonecutter and mason, to carve fourteen stone heads for the front of the building. The heads were erected on stone columns in 1669, though it is not known whom the heads represent. They are known by many names including the

Emperors' Heads, the Faceless Caesars, the Philosophers and the Twelve Apostles and may represent emperors, gods or wise men. They were carved in good Headington stone and lasted two hundred years before they needed replacing. In fact, due to the construction of the Clarendon Building there was only room for thirteen of them to be replaced. However, these replacements were carved from poor quality Headington stone, which by the middle of the 20th century needed replacing again. So worn were they that John Betjeman compared them with 'illustrations in a medical textbook on skin diseases'. In 1970 they were taken down, and new heads, weighing about a ton each, and carved in Clipsham stone by Michael Black, were erected over the next two years. They were based, as far as possible, on the originals, although only eleven of them could be traced (mainly to private gardens around Oxford), and each has a beard, which has led Michael Black to state that they represent a history of beards.

The theatre can often be seen in passing in various *Inspector Morse* and *Lewis* episodes and did feature in its own right in *Lewis: Falling Darkness*, but it will always be remembered for its role in *Twilight of the Gods*, in which the obnoxious suave and rich Andrew Baydon is due to be awarded an honorary Doctorate of Law by the University of Oxford in the Sheldonian Theatre. On the *Encaenia* walk towards the theatre, he is accompanied by the opera diva Gwladys Probert, who is shot by an unknown assassin; but was the bullet really meant for her or for him?

TOWN HALL

The current building was not the first Town Hall on this site. It was in 1229 that King Henry III sold to the burgesses a house on the east side of St. Aldate's for use as a courtroom. The house was altered extensively during the 13th century and around 1550 the freehold of an adjoining house was gained and became the lower Guildhall. More alterations and improvements were carried out to both houses in the 16th and 17th centuries. The Guildhall was demolished in 1751 and a new Town Hall, designed by Isaac Ware, built in the classical style. This building incorporated the General Post Office with Nixon's Free Grammar School behind, and behind that the Corn Exchange.

The foundation stone of the present Town Hall was laid on 6th July 1893. The building, designed by Henry T. Hare, is partly Jacobean in style and was opened by the Prince of Wales, later King Edward VII, on 12th May 1897. The façade is symmetrical, except for the south turret, with a balcony over the entrance from which results of parliamentary elections are announced to those in St. Aldate's. Originally the south corner was a library, but is now occupied by the Museum of Oxford, which in 1997 hosted an Inspector Morse exhibition.

Beneath the Town Hall is a 14th or 15th century vaulted crypt which houses the City Plate collection. The building also has a courtroom that was used as a magistrates' court, for Quarter Sessions, and as a Crown Court until 1985, when a new Crown Court building was opened opposite the police station further down St. Aldates. A grand staircase leads to the main hall, which boasts an original Henry Willis organ. Throughout the building will be found many fine paintings, arms and carved heads of those associated with the city.

[The Town Hall]

According to *The Jewel that was Ours* (based on *The Wolvercote Tongue*) a wartime hop held in the Town Hall was the first meeting place of Howard Brown and Betty Fowler. Since 1945, the Atlantic Ocean and their own marriages had separated them. Howard Brown and his wife travel to Oxford on 'the historic cities of England tour' and he manages to sneak off for a brief re-union with Betty at the University Parks.

It is the ballroom, though, that is most memorable as the place where Morse gets to dance with Dr. Grayling Russell in *The Secret of Bay 5B*. However, much of the interior was in fact filmed in London. The Town Hall does make further appearances, though, in *Lewis: The Quality of Mercy* and *Lewis: The Dead of Winter* where it doubles both times as the courthouse and courtroom.

TRINITY COLLEGE

|Perhaps the best aspect of Trinity College is from The Grove|

Trinity College was founded by Sir Thomas Pope in 1555. He was a devout Catholic with no surviving children who saw the foundation of an Oxford college as a means of ensuring that he and his family name would always be remembered in the prayers and masses of its members. He came from a family of small landowners in Oxfordshire, trained as a

93

lawyer, and rose rapidly to prominence under King Henry VIII. As Treasurer of the Court of Augmentations he handled the estates of the monasteries dissolved at the Reformation, and amassed a considerable personal fortune. Later he became a discreet and trusted privy counsellor of Mary Tudor, and it was from Mary and Philip that he received Letters Patent and royal approval for his new foundation. The statutes of the college set out rules for a simple monastic life of religious observance and study, with a garden comprising an informal grove of trees, mainly elms, amongst which the members of the college could walk and meditate.

In fact Trinity College was not a new college at all, for in 1554 Pope merely purchased what remained of Durham College, a former monastic college which had fallen victim to the dissolution, and its simple buildings sufficed for the next hundred years. Pope died in 1559 and is the only founder of either an Oxford or Cambridge college to lie under a monument in his own foundation. Today the Old Library dating from 1421 is the only building that survives from the former Durham College.

In 1618 the then President undertook to build a cellar under the refectory but this collapsed and as a consequence the present Hall was constructed. The Civil War saw the college empty of scholars and all the college silver being given over to the king to be turned into coin to pay the troops. By the end of the war the college was virtually bankrupt, although fortunes were to return with thanks to one of the Fellows, Ralph Bathurst, who recognised a need to attract the aristocracy to Oxford. He had his friend, one Christopher Wren, design some luxurious accommodation for students (which included rooms for their servants) along what is today part of the Garden Quadrangle. The two-storey building was completed in 1668, but soon more accommodation was needed, so a second building was added in the 1680s. At the same time the garden became more formal, with an avenue of lime trees, a complex pattern of paths, obelisks and a maze. Indeed, the college has seen a gradual expansion of its buildings and increased student numbers ever since.

In the 18th century Trinity College was at the forefront of reform and in 1789 introduced a simple form of examination, although women had to wait until 1979 to be admitted. Among the famous alumni are John Aubrey, Sir Richard Burton, Miles Kington, William Pitt the Elder and Terrence Rattigan.

As far as filming goes, it was featured in *The Last Enemy*, *The Wench is Dead*, in which Dr. Van Buren walks and talks with Kershaw, and *Twilight of the Gods*, as the setting for the reception with Sir John

Gielgud. It has also made several *Lewis* appearances. In *Lewis: Music to Die For* it became Saville College, while in *Lewis: Falling Darkness* it was the location of Belisarius's flat, and finally to date it returned for a second time as Saville College in *Lewis: The Gift of Promise*.

TURF TAVERN

[The Turf Tavern]

Situated between St. Helen's Passage and Bath Place, the Turf Tavern, probably the most famous of Oxford's public houses, started as a malt house. Later it became a cider house in 1775, and finally an inn, the Spotted Cow, around 1790. Building land within the Oxford city wall was scarce at this time, so many small tenements were erected just outside it.

The Spotted Cow became the Turf Tavern in 1847 and has remained open as an inn, with the exception of a small period in 1986 and 1987 when there was a dispute concerning the will of the late landlord, who had run it for over thirty years. To this day it has remained ever popular with tourists and students alike. The timber-framed building, the original now long gone, is actually on lease from Merton College.

In the book *The Daughters of Cain* Morse and Lewis travel to Leicester to visit Mary Rodway to talk about her son's drug-related suicide. On their return to Oxford they go to the Turf Tavern for a drink. It also features in *The Settling of the Sun* and most importantly has the honour as being the only place where Morse refuses a drink from Lewis, having just spotted Ruth Rawlinson (whom he tries to court) with Harry Josephs here in *Service of All the Dead*. There is even a blackboard-style plaque commemorating the link between Inspector Morse and this award-winning public house, which in 2007 became the national winner of the perfect pub award.

To date this popular establishment has only made a single *Lewis* appearance, in *Lewis: And Moonbeams Kiss the Sea* as part of Nell Buckley's alternative secret Oxford tour where she reveals that 'allegedly' J. R. R. Tolkien was a member of a jazz band and played the banjo here.

TURL STREET

This is an ancient street running between Broad Street and High Street. It gets its name from a revolving (twirling) gate which was in a postern in the city wall at the Broad Street end. It was demolished in 1722. Almost the whole of the east side of the street is taken up by Exeter and Lincoln Colleges, while the west side has a row of mainly late 18th century stucco and timber-framed houses, along with Jesus College. The television episode entitled *The Last Enemy* has Lewis calling on a tailor (Walters, founded in 1887) in Turl Street for help in identifying a 'suited torso' found in the canal at Thrupp.

[Turl Street as seen from High Street]

Outside he happens upon the pathologist, Dr. Grayling Russell, and they walk along the street, discussing Morse's toothache and an appropriate present for a godchild. Filming took place here for *Deadly Slumber* and *The Way Through the Woods*, in which the Past Times shop became a bookshop.

Lewis and Hathaway visit the Turl Bar in *Lewis: Life Born of Fire* while in *Lewis: The Point of Vanishing* it is here at the junction with Brasenose Lane that a car swerves and honks as Hathaway and Madeleine Cotton walk along the street. Turl Street and the Turl Bar also appear briefly in *Lewis: Counter Culture Blues*. There is a further shot of the street in *Lewis: Falling Darkness* in which Laura Hobson is on her way to the Turl Club (in real life the Corner Club located at No. 16 Turl Street). The Oxfam bookshop in Turl Street doubles as the rare bookshop in *Lewis: The Dead of Winter*, while Turl Street News appears in *Lewis: The Mind Has Mountains*, and finally the Missing Bean Café features in *Lewis: Wild Justice*.

Turl Street was also seen in *Lewis: Whom the Gods Would Destroy*, while in the same episode Bundrick's Bicycles (actually Bike Zone, a well-known Oxford business but sadly now gone) is located close to the corner of Turl Street and Market Street.

[**Bundrick's Bicycles**]

UNIVERSITY COLLEGE

University College, commonly known as 'Univ.', was the first collegiate foundation in Oxford, and was bequeathed by William of Durham in 1249. The intention was to buy property, the rents from which would maintain up to a dozen Masters of Arts studying divinity. The first buildings were acquired in 1253 (University Hall) with others following in 1280. In fact University College may not be the founding college since although it had the first benefactor, Balliol College had the first actual site and Merton College the first statutes.

The entire college was excommunicated in 1411 for supporting the Lollard heresies, and the Master and Fellows were again expelled during the Civil War. In 1380 there was a land dispute in which the college was likely to lose everything, but the Fellows petitioned the Crown asserting that the college had been founded by King Alfred, and that therefore the current monarch was also the protector of the establishment. The spurious claim was upheld and to this day King Alfred is prayed for on college feast days. The place is not without a sense of humour, for in 1872 the college celebrated its millennium and was presented with a parcel of burnt cakes at the celebratory dinner by the then Regius Professor of History.

University College has always been fortunate in having rich benefactors who allowed the college to keep increasing in size, and with that came academic distinction. Currently it is among the five or six leading colleges in academic and intellectual standing in Great Britain.

Unfortunately no buildings earlier than 1634 survive, and much of the current college is in the Gothic style with little of architectural note, especially since the original limestone was of poor quality and after only one hundred and sixty years needed replacing, which was done in a much simpler way, dispensing with pinnacles and other ornamentation.

Among the college's distinguished members are Leonard Digges (inventor of the theodolite), Percy Bysshe Shelley, K. A. Busia (Prime Minister of Ghana), R. J. L. Hawke (Prime Minister of Australia), C. S. Lewis, Professor Stephen Hawking and the British Prime Ministers Clement Attlee and Harold Wilson. Finally, although not Fellows, the scientists Robert Boyle (sometimes described as the first modern chemist) and his assistant Robert Hooke (architect, biologist and discoverer of cells) lived in Deep Hall and conducted various experiments here.

[Memorial to 'one of the guys in the band']

A specially constructed building in the college, the Shelley Memorial, built on what was Deep Hall, houses a statue by Edward Onslow Ford of Percy Bysshe Shelley, who was expelled for writing *The Necessity of Atheism*. He is depicted lying dead on the Italian seashore. Rumour has it that the sunken area around the statue was once filled with water and populated by live goldfish as a student prank. Another apparently common student prank involving the statue has been to paint his genitalia bright colours; cleaning has rendered the statue's appendage somewhat smaller than it used to be.

Although Inspector Morse never visited the college for filming, the same is not true of Lewis and Hathaway, for in *Lewis: And the Moonbeams Kiss the Sea* good use is made of the Shelley Memorial, and again in *Lewis: Allegory of Love* the rooms of Dorian Crane, Hamid Jassim and Melanie Harding are all within the college, while in *Lewis: The Mind Has Mountains* this is the location of Eagleton's rooms and the Dean's lodgings.

WADHAM COLLEGE

[Entrance to Wadham College]

The college was in principle founded upon the instruction, and funding, of Nicholas Wadham upon his deathbed in 1609, but really it was his wife, Dorothy, who was the true founder, for it was she who acquired the land (an old priory of Augustinian Friars) in 1610 (having negotiated the price down from £1,000 to £600). She oversaw the building work, which cost around £26,000 and which today affords one of the finest examples of this period, most notably the fine stone-vaulted gateway and equally spacious quadrangle.

The Hall is also one of Oxford's finest architecturally and maybe gave inspiration to Sir Christopher Wren, who was a Member at the college. It became a relatively poor place to study following the Civil War, in which it chose the wrong side to support (along with most of Oxford). In 1648 John Wilkins was appointed Warden, and he attracted a distinguished set of scientific Fellows. The college's future was secured when Wilkins married Oliver Cromwell's sister although, there were many financial ups and downs in the centuries that followed.

By the early 20th century Wadham was considered a modest but respectable place, catering for the less-affluent professional classes, with around one hundred Members. It later became one of the first colleges to open its doors to women.

The college was used in the filming of *Who Killed Harry Field?*, *The Daughters of Cain*, *The Wench is Dead* and was also the centre of action for *Lewis: Reputation*, where it was the location of Danny's student room, Denniston's lecture room and the exterior of what the location sheet simply described as 'a pretty place ... Wadham College gardens?'. That it certainly is! Most recently it had a small role as the exterior of the Suskin Press in *Lewis: The Gift of Promise*.

WHITE HORSE PUBLIC HOUSE

The White Horse at No. 52 Broad Street is sandwiched between two branches of Blackwell's bookshop. It is a small two-roomed 18th century timber-framed tavern, although the frontage was completely rebuilt in 1951.

Morse has a drink here with Anne Staveley in *The Dead of Jericho*, and again drinks here in *The Secret of Bay 5B*, when he is clever enough to work out the rather obvious invitation from Dr. Grayling Russell for lunch. However, on that occasion he runs off when he sees Janice, Gifford's (the murdered architect's) receptionist. It also has an appearance in *The Wolvercote Tongue*. It seems strange, but from the films perspective this must be a quiet part of town, rather than the very centre, for Morse has no trouble finding a parking space right outside this public house!

[The White Horse public house]

More recently Lewis visits here in *Lewis: Allegory of Love*, *Lewis: Old, Unhappy, Far Off Things*, and also *Lewis: Counter Culture Blues*, where it masquerades as The Kings Arms (which is strange, since in reality The Kings Arms is only a few paces away at the end of Broad Street).

INSPECTOR MORSE MAP

The following map is merely intended to show the relative positions of the various locations covered in the text and is not meant to be to scale. The associated table gives the type of place according to the defined symbols below, along with the page number in brackets for that location. In so doing it is hoped that the maps will help readers when planning their own visits to these places of interest. Please note that the Cherwell Boat House, Lady Margaret Hall, Park Town and the Radcliffe Observatory are all located outside the main city centre and so not included here.

Key to Symbols

Building (general)	Building (large or important)	Church (religious establishment)
Museum (other tourist attraction)	Park (garden or open space)	Place of Learning (college or library)
Public House (or hotel/restaurant)	Shop (or market)	

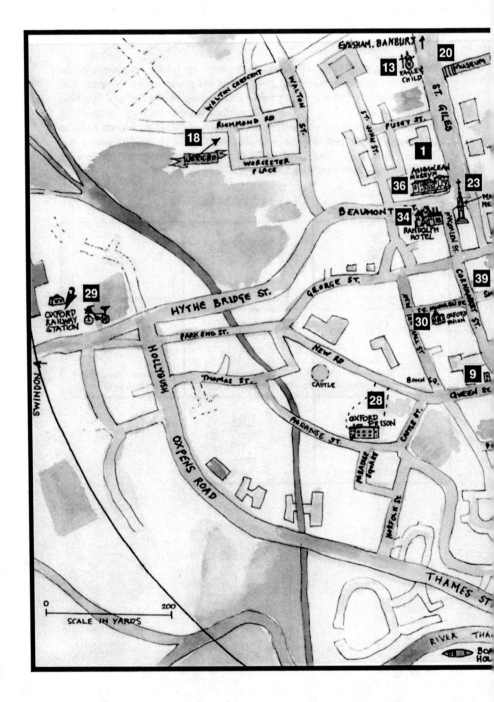

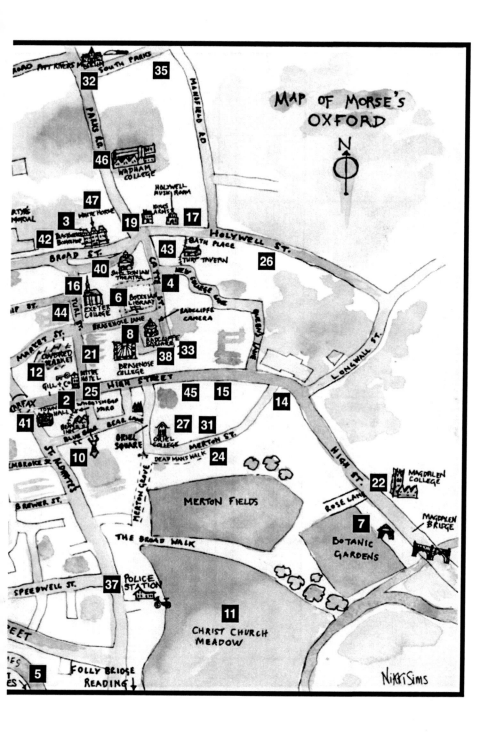

Key to Map

1	Ashmolean Museum (9)		2	Bear Inn (12)	
3	Blackwell's Bookshop (13)		4	Bridge of Sighs (14)	
5	Boathouses (15)		6	Bodleian Library (16)	
7	Botanic Gardens (20)		8	Brasenose College (22)	
9	Carfax (25)		10	Christ Church College (27)	
11	Christ Church Meadow (27)		12	Covered Market (30)	
13	Eagle & Child (32)		14	Eastgate Hotel (33)	
15	Examination Halls (34)		16	Exeter College (35)	
17	Holywell Music Room (37)		18	Jericho (39)	

19	King's Arms (42)	20	Lamb & Flag (44)
21	Lincoln College (45)	22	Magdalen College (47)
23	Martyrs' Memorial (50)	24	Merton College (52)
25	Mitre Hotel (25)	26	New College (26)
27	Oriel College & Square (27)	28	Oxford Prison (28)
29	Oxford Railway Station (64)	30	Oxford Union (67)
31	Oxford University Real Tennis Club (69)	32	Pitt Rivers & University Museums (71)
33	Radcliffe Camera (75)	34	Randolph Hotel (78)
35	Rothermere American Institute (81)	36	Sackler Library (82)

37	St. Aldates Police Station (84)		38	St. Mary the Virgin (85)	
39	St. Michael's at the North Gate (88)		40	Sheldonian Theatre (89)	
41	Town Hall (91)		42	Trinity College (93)	
43	Turf Tavern (95)		44	Turl Street (96)	
45	University College (97)		46	Wadham College (99)	
47	White Horse (100)				

INSPECTOR MORSE WALKING TOUR

The following is a suggested Inspector Morse walking tour, which being circular may be joined at any point and taken in any direction. The walk should take around three hours to complete (but please do allow extra time for refreshments and to actually enter some of these wonderful locations). Where appropriate, admission charges are shown but, although most of the colleges do now charge an admission, often if you just want to take a photograph for a couple of minutes and have a friendly word with the staff, they will often let you enter for free. The numbers in brackets refer to the location map in the previous section. Please note that the Cherwell Boat House, Lady Margaret Hall, Park Town and the Radcliffe Observatory were deemed too far outside the main city centre and so are not included in this walking tour.

Step 1
Oxford Railway Station **(29)** ⇐10 minutes⇒ Oxford Prison **(28)**

From Park End Street walk to New Road (admission charge for castle attraction)

Step 2
Oxford Prison **(28)** ⇐5 minutes⇒ Carfax **(9)**

From New Road walk to Queen Street which comes to Carfax (admission charge to climb tower)

Step 3
Carfax **(28)** ⇐2 minutes⇒ Town Hall **(41)**

From Carfax continue to St. Aldate's (small but interesting museum on Oxford city)

Step 4
Town Hall **(41)** ⇐2 minutes⇒ Christ Church College **(10)**

Continue down St. Aldate's (admission charge)

Step 5
Christ Church College **(10)** ⇐2 minutes⇒ St. Aldates Police Station **(37)**

Continue down St. Aldate's (note Inspector Morse plaque)

107

Step 6
St. Aldate's Police Station **(37)** ⬅20 minutes➡ Boat Houses **(5)**

From St. Aldate's continue to Folly Bridge and take tow path on left (nice walk but have to return the same way so optional)

Step 7
Boat Houses **(5)** ⬅20 minutes➡ Christ Church Meadow **(11)**

Return along tow path to Folly Bridge and up St. Aldate's to The Broad Walk gates on the right

Step 8
Christ Church Meadow **(11)** ⬅5 minutes➡ Botanic Gardens **(7)**

Walk along The Broad Walk to Rose Lane at far side and up to High Street turning right for main entrance to Botanic Gardens (admission charge)

Step 9
Botanic Gardens **(7)** ⬅0 minutes➡ Magdalen College & Bridge **(22)**

Opposite Botanic Gardens (admission charge for college)

Step 10
Magdalen College & Bridge **(22)** ⬅2 minutes➡ Eastgate Hotel **(14)**

Continue on up High Street

Step 11
Eastgate Hotel **(14)** ⬅1 minute➡ Examination Halls **(15)**

Continue on up High Street (not open to the public)

Step 12
Examination Halls **(15)** ⬅1 minute➡ University College **(45)**

Continue on up High Street (admission charge)

Step 13
University College **(45)** ⬅4 minutes➡ Oxford Uni. Real Tennis Club **(31)**

From High Street take Logic Lane on the left to Merton Street and then turn right (private club but staff are usually happy to let visitors in)

Step 14
Oxford Uni. Real Tennis Club **(31)** ⬅0 minutes➡ Merton College **(24)**

Almost opposite in Merton Street (admission charge)

Step 15
Merton College (24) ⇦1 minute⇨ Oriel College & Square (27)
Continue up Merton Street to Oriel Square (admission charge)

Step 16
Oriel College & Square (27) ⇦1 minute⇨ Bear Inn (2)
Oriel Square to Bear Lane (don't forget to go inside and look at the ties)

Step 17
Bear Inn (2) ⇦1 minute⇨ Mitre Hotel (25)
Bear Lane to Blue Boar Court to High Street (the Mitre Hotel is opposite)

Step 18
Mitre Hotel (25) ⇦1 minute⇨ Covered Market (12)
Almost next to the Mitre Hotel in High Street is an entrance to the Covered Market (the cake shop is especially interesting)

Step 19
Covered Market (12) ⇦4 minutes⇨ St. Michael at the North Gate (39)
Exit other side of Covered Market to Market Street then up to Cornmarket Street and turn right (admission charge to go up tower)

Step 20
St. Michael at the North Gate (39) ⇦1 minute⇨ Oxford Union (30)
Cornmarket Street to St. Michael's Street opposite (not open to the public)

Step 21
Oxford Union (30) ⇦8 minutes⇨ Sackler Library (36)
Right at bottom of St. Michael's Street to New Inn Hall Street and straight over George Street to St. George's Place and keep going straight to Gloucester Street and Beaumont Street, where almost opposite is St. John Street and the Sackler Library close to the corner (not open to the public) while further down on right is Wendy Spencer's house

Step 22
Sackler Library (36) ⇦1 minute⇨ Ashmolean Museum (1)
From St. John Street continue up Beaumont Street (free admission and lovely roof garden restaurant)

Step 23
Ashmolean Museum **(1)** ⇐0 minutes⇒ Randolph Hotel **(34)**
Opposite Ashmolean Museum. The Morse Bar is on the left as you enter

Step 24
Randolph Hotel **(34)** ⇐2 minutes⇒ Martyrs' Memorial **(23)**
On corner opposite Randolph Hotel in St. Giles'

Step 25
Martyrs' Memorial **(23)** ⇐2 minutes⇒ Trinity College **(42)**
Take Magdalen Street East and turn left Broad Street (admission charge)

Step 26
Trinity College **(42)** ⇐1 minute⇒ Blackwell's Bookshop **(3)**
Continue down Broad Street

Step 27
Blackwell's Bookshop **(3)** ⇐0 minutes⇒ White Horse **(47)**
Sandwiched between the two main Blackwell's Bookshop sites

Step 28
White Horse **(47)** ⇐0 minutes⇒ Sheldonian Theatre **(40)**
Opposite the White Horse in Broad Street (admission charge)

Step 29
Sheldonian Theatre **(40)** ⇐0 minutes⇒ Bodleian Library **(6)**
Adjacent to the Sheldonian Theatre (admission charge)

Step 30
Bodleian Library **(6)** ⇐2 minutes⇒ Exeter College **(16)**
Retrace your steps up Broad Street and turn left into Turl Street (admission charge)

Step 31
Exeter College **(16)** ⇐1 minute⇒ Lincoln College **(21)**
Continue down Turl Street (admission charge)

Step 32

Lincoln College **(21)** ⬅2 minutes⮕ Turl Street **(44)**

You are already in Turl Street but the locations filmed are further down towards High Street on the right

Step 33

Turl Street **(44)** ⬅2 minutes⮕ Radcliffe Square **(33)**

Retrace your route along Turl Street and turn right in Brasenose Lane which leads to Radcliffe Square (no public entry)

Step 34

Radcliffe Square **(33)** ⬅0 minutes⮕ Brasenose College **(8)**

In Radcliffe Square to your immediate right (admission charge)

Step 35

Brasenose College **(8)** ⬅0 minutes⮕ St. Mary the Virgin **(38)**

Along south side of Radcliffe Square (admission charge to climb tower)

Step 36

St. Mary the Virgin **(38)** ⬅2 minutes⮕ Bridge of Sighs **(4)**

From Radcliffe Square take Catte Street, the Bridge of Sighs is in New College Lane on your right

Step 37

Bridge of Sighs **(4)** ⬅1 minute⮕ Turf Tavern **(43)**

Just by Bridge of Sighs alley leads to Turf Tavern

Step 38

Turf Tavern **(43)** ⬅1 minute⮕ Holywell Music Room **(17)**

Exit via Bath Place and Holywell Music Room is opposite

Step 39

Holywell Music Room **(17)** ⬅1 minute⮕ New College **(26)**

Continue down Holywell Street (admission charge)

Step 40

New College **(26)** ⬅2 minutes⮕ King's Arms **(19)**

Retrace your steps past the Holywell Music Room to Broad Street

Step 41

King's Arms **(19)** ⇦1 minute⇨ Wadham College **(46)**

Turn right into Parks Road (admission charge)

Step 42

Wadham College **(46)** ⇦5 minutes⇨ Rothermere American Inst. **(35)**

Continue along Parks Road and turn right into South Parks Road and continue until you come to the junction with Mansfield Road

Step 43

Rothermere American Inst. **(35)** ⇦1 minute⇨ Pitt Rivers & Uni.

Museums **(32)**

Retrace your steps to Parks Road and turn right (free admission)

Step 44

Pitt Rivers & Uni. Museums **(32)** ⇦2 minutes⇨ Lamb & Flag **(20)**

Take Museum Road opposite and continue up passage

Step 45

Lamb & Flag **(20)** ⇦0 minutes⇨ Eagle & Child **(13)**

Directly opposite

Step 46

Eagle & Child **(13)** ⇦30 minutes⇨ Jericho **(18)**

Continue up St. Giles' and branch left into the Woodstock Road before turning left into Little Clarendon Street. At Walton Street continue straight over in Walton Crescent and at the end turn right into Nelson Street. Continue down Nelson Street noting No. 31 and then turn right into Canal Street. Opposite the Old Bookbinders is Coombe Road on the left. From here take Victor Street at the side of the Old Bookbinders and then go straight across Albert Street into Jericho Street which leads back up to Walton Street. The Phoenix cinema is on your left.

Step 47

Jericho **(18)** ⇦20 minutes⇨ Oxford Railway Station **(29)**

From the Phoenix cinema go back along Walton Road past the Jericho public house and the Oxford University Press to the junction with Worcester Street on your right. Follow the road around to Hythe Bridge Street which goes into Park End Street and leads to the railway station.

112

PLACES INDEX

113

114

Public House (Hotel or Restaurant)

Shop (or Market)

EPISODE INDEX

Inspector Morse

Lewis

Endeavour

REFERENCES & FURTHER READING

Allen, Paul & Allen, Jan, *Endeavouring to Crack the Morse Code*, Lightning Source UK Limited, (2006), ISBN: 978 1846855 11 5, 371 pages. Interesting subject matter but appallingly written and produced with literally hundreds of errors.

Bird, Christopher, *The World of Inspector Morse*, Boxtree, (1998), ISBN: 978 0752221 17 5, 160 pages. A complete A-Z reference for the Morse enthusiast with foreword by Colin Dexter. Several mistakes but still remains one of the best guides to Inspector Morse available.

Bishop, David, *The Complete Inspector Morse*, Reynolds and Hearn Limited, (2009), ISBN: 978 1905287 91 8, 319 pages. Attempts to be the last word on Inspector Morse containing a critique of all the novels, television adaptations, and other writers' stories featuring the popular characters. A default guide for any enthusiast.

Bullen, Annie, *Morse in Oxford*, Pitkin Publishing, (2009), ISBN: 978 1841652 27 6, 33 pages. At just 34 pages a rather lightweight guide to Inspector Morse though as with all Pitkin publications very well illustrated, but with nothing new that cannot be found elsewhere, including the music CD which comes with the booklet. The *Lewis* series is completely ignored.

Earwaker, Julian & Becker, Kathleen, *Scene of the Crime*, Aurum Press, (2002), ISBN: 978 1854108 21 0, 256 pages. A superb work surveying the landscapes of British detective fiction. Although broad in content this guide is not comprehensive within a particular author or location.

Godwin, John, & Richards, Antony *The Murder of Christina Collins*, Irregular Special Press, (2011), ISBN: 978 1901091 44 1, 59 pages. Definitive guide to the real life murder of Christina Collins on the Trent and Mersey Canal at Rugeley, Staffordshire in 1839. It was upon this event that Colin Dexter based his book *The Wench Is Dead*. This expanded version with an introduction by Colin Dexter also includes a useful gazetteer to all the locations of interest.

Goodwin, Cliff, *Inspector Morse Country*, Headline Book Publishing (Hodder Headline*)*, (2002), ISBN: 978 0755310 64 7, 224 pages. A beautifully produced tribute to the world of Oxford's famous detective. Well illustrated with many useful addresses and other information. An essential part of any Inspector Morse collection.

Hibbert, Christopher (Editor) & Hibbert, Edward (Associate Editor), *The Encyclopaedia of Oxford*, Macmillan London Limited, (1988), ISBN: 978 0333486 14 6, 562 pages. Essential reading for anybody interested in the history of Oxford.

Honey, Derek, *An Encyclopaedia of Oxford Pubs, Inns and Taverns*, Oakwood Press, (1998), ISBN: 978 0853615 35 4, 128 pages. An informative guide, with foreword by Colin Dexter, to over 700 establishments along with mention of those most frequented by Inspector Morse.

Leonard, Bill, *The Oxford of Inspector Morse and Lewis*, The History Press, (2008), ISBN: 978 0752446 21 9, 224 pages. Despite being full of information, often minutiae, relating to Inspector Morse and Oxford it is poorly produced and relies heavily on information already published elsewhere. The text is set out non-logically, the photographs amateurish and much is copied from an earlier publication. Such a pity as this should have been the definitive guide to Inspector Morse locations. Only the early *Lewis* episodes mentioned.

Richards, Antony, *Inspector Morse on Location*, (2011), ISBN 978 1901091 30 4, 112 pages. This expanded companion to *The Oxford of Inspector Morse* and the default guide to over 75 places outside Oxford city centre that were used in filming *Inspector Morse* and *Lewis*, fully illustrated and with location maps.

Sanderson, Mark, *The Making of Inspector Morse*, Macmillan London Limited, (1991), ISBN 978 0330344 18 0, 144 pages. A classic guide to the filming of the series that should be on every Inspector Morse enthusiast's shelf.

All the photographs in this publication are by Antony J. Richards. The line illustrations on pages 18, 21, 29, 39, 48 and 86 are taken from *Old England: a pictorial Museum of Royal, Ecclesiastical, Municipal, Baronial, and popular Antiquities* edited by Charles Knight and printed in the middle of the 19th century by *James Sangster & Co.*, Paternoster Row, London. The line illustration on page 50 is taken from *A Hand-Book for Visitors to Oxford*, 1847. The illustrations on pages 13 and 79 are taken from original advertisements by kind permission from Blackwell's and the Randolph Hotel respectively. The illustration on page 74 is by permission of the Pitt Rivers Museum.

CPSIA information can be obtained at www.ICGtesting.com
Printed in the USA
BVOW02s1314130115

383139BV00008B/45/P

9 781901 091038